Horizons

Phonics and Reading

K

Teacher's Guide 4
Lessons 121–160

Author: Pollyann O'Brien, M.A.

Editor: Alan L. Christopherson, M.S.

Alpha Omega Publications, Inc. • Rock Rapids, IA

© MM by Alpha Omega Publications, Inc. ® All rights reserved.
804 N. 2nd Ave. E., Rock Rapids, IA 51246-1759
800-622-3070   www.aop.com

Printed in the United States of America

ISBN 978-0-7403-0308-1

Scope & Sequence

Lesson 1

Letter **a**
- letter recognition
- short **a** sound
- recognizing and forming upper-case and lower-case **a**

Lesson 2

Letter **b**
- letter recognition
- beginning and ending letter **b** sound
- sound of **ba**
- recognizing and forming upper-case and lower-case **b**

Lesson 3

Letter **d**
- letter recognition
- letter **d** sound
- sound of **dă**
- recognizing and forming upper-case and lower-case **d**

Lesson 4

Letter **o**
- letter recognition
- beginning sound of short **o**
- recognizing and forming upper-case and lower-case **o**
- sound of **lŏ**
- words with short **o** in the middle
- formation of **ba, bo, do, dad**

Lesson 5

Letter **c**
- letter recognition
- sound of letter **c**
- words beginning with **c** and **că**
- recognizing and forming upper-case and lower-case **c**
- formation of **co, ca**

Lesson 6

Letter **e**
- letter recognition
- sound of short **e**
- words with **ĕ** in the middle
- matching phrases to pictures
- beginning sounds **dĕ** and **bĕ**
- word recognition and matching
- recognizing and forming upper-case and lower-case **e**
- matching letter to pictures starting with **ĕ**

Lesson 7

Letter **f**
- letter recognition
- sound of **f**
- beginning sounds **f, fă, fĕ**
- recognizing and forming upper-case and lower-case **f**
- reading and writing "make-up words"
- reading and writing short sentences

Lesson 8

Letter **g**
- letter recognition
- beginning sounds **g, gă, gŏ**
- words beginning and ending in **g**
- auditory discrimination from word list
- recognizing and forming upper-case and lower-case **g**
- matching letter to pictures starting with **g**
- reading and writing "make-up words"
- reading and writing short sentences

Lesson 9

Letter **i**
- letter recognition
- beginning sound of short **i**
- words with short **i** in the middle
- beginning consonant sounds
- middle vowel sounds
- recognizing and forming upper-case and lower-case **i**
- matching letter to pictures starting with **i**

Lesson 10

Letter **h**

- letter recognition
- beginning sounds **h**, **hă**, **hĕ**, **hŏ**, **hĭ**
- recognizing and forming upper-case and lower-case **h**
- reading and writing "make-up words"
- matching letter to pictures starting with **h**
- adding **s** to make plurals
- capital letter at beginning and period at end of sentence
- matching pictures to phrases

Lesson 11

Letter **u**

- letter recognition
- beginning sounds of **ŭ**, **dŭ**, **fŭ**, **bŭ**, **cŭ**, **gŭ**
- words with **ŭ** in the middle
- recognizing and forming upper-case and lower-case **u**
- matching letter to pictures with **ŭ** in the middle
- matching pictures to words

Lesson 12

Letter **t**

- letter recognition
- beginning and ending sound of **t**
- recognizing and forming upper-case and lower-case **t**
- matching letter to pictures starting with **t**
- reading and writing "make-up words"
- reading and printing sentences
- matching pictures to phrases
- recognition and printing **ta**, **te**, **ti**, **to**, **tu**

Lesson 13

Letter **n**

- letter recognition
- sound of **n**, **nă**
- matching pictures to words
- recognizing and forming upper-case and lower-case **n**

- matching letters to words starting with **n**
- spelling words to match pictures
- completing sentences with correct word
- printing words and phrases from copy
- identifying pictures starting with **ne**, **ni**, **nu**, **no**
- identifying pictures starting with **an**, **en**, **in**, **un**

Lesson 14

Letter **k**

- letter recognition
- beginning sounds **k**, **kĭ**, **kĕ**
- matching pictures to phrases
- recognizing and forming upper-case and lower-case **k**
- printing letters and words with **k**
- reading "make-up words"
- reading and printing sentences

Lesson 15

Letter **l**

- letter recognition
- beginning sounds **l**, **lă**, **lĕ**, **lĭ**, **lŏ**, **lŭ**
- ending sound of **l**
- recognizing and forming upper-case and lower-case **l**
- printing letters and words
- completing sentences with correct word
- reading "make-up words"

Lesson 16

Letter **m**

- recognizing and forming upper-case and lower-case **m**
- completing sentences with correct word
- spelling words to match pictures
- reading "make-up words"
- matching pictures to beginning sounds **ma**, **me**, **mi**, **mo**, **mu**
- reading and printing words and phrases from copy

Lesson 17

Letter **p**
- recognizing and forming upper-case and lower-case **p**
- beginning sounds of **pa**, **pe**, **pi**, **po**, **pu**
- matching pictures to words
- matching letters to words starting with **p**
- reading "make-up words"
- spelling words to match pictures
- printing words and phrases from copy
- completing sentences with correct word

Lesson 18

Letter **r**
- recognizing and forming upper-case and lower-case **r**
- matching letters to words starting with **r**
- reading "make-up words"
- beginning sounds of **ra**, **re**, **ri**, **ro**, **ru**
- matching pictures to words
- completing sentences with correct word
- spelling words to match pictures
- printing words and phrases from copy

Lesson 19

Letter **s**
- recognizing and forming upper-case and lower-case **s**
- matching letters to words starting with **s**
- beginning sounds of **sa**, **se**, **si**, **so**, **su**
- matching pictures to phrases
- recognizing ending sound of **s**
- printing letters, words, and phrases
- completing sentences with correct word

Lesson 20

Letter **q**
- recognizing and forming upper-case and lower-case **q**, **qu**, **qui**
- matching letters to words starting with **qu**
- match pictures to words
- reading and writing sentences

Lesson 21

Letter **j**
- recognizing and forming upper-case and lower-case **j**
- matching letters to words starting with **j**
- matching pictures to words
- completing sentences with correct word
- matching pictures to phrases
- beginning sounds of **ja**, **je**, **ji**, **jo**, **ju**
- spelling words to match pictures
- printing words and phrases from copy

Lesson 22

Letter **v**
- recognizing and forming upper-case and lower-case **v**
- matching letters to words starting with **v**
- spelling words to match pictures
- matching pictures to words and phrases
- beginning sounds of **va**, **ve**, **vi**, **vo**, **vu**
- completing sentences with correct word
- printing words and phrases from copy
- spelling words to match pictures

Lesson 23

Letter **w**
- recognizing and forming upper-case and lower-case **w**
- matching letters to words starting with **w**
- reading "make-up words"
- matching pictures to words and phrases
- printing words from copy
- completing sentences with correct word
- spelling words to match pictures
- reading and printing sentences

Lesson 24

Letter **y**
- recognizing and forming upper-case and lower-case **y**
- printing letters and words
- matching letters to words starting with **y**
- matching pictures to words and phrases

- completing sentences with correct word
- spelling words to match pictures

Lesson 25

Letter **z**

- recognizing and forming upper-case and lower-case **z**
- matching letters to words starting with **z**
- matching pictures to words
- reading "make-up words"
- recognizing words that end in **z**
- printing letters and words
- completing sentences with correct word
- printing phrases from copy

Lesson 26

Letter **x**

- recognizing and forming upper-case and lower-case **x**
- matching letters to words starting with **x**
- reading "make-up words"
- matching pictures to phrases, sentences, words
- words ending in **x**
- completing sentences with correct word
- spelling words to match pictures
- printing phrases from copy

Lesson 27

Consonant digraph **th**

- rule for beginning consonant digraph **th**
- matching picture to starting sound of **th**
- printing upper-case/lower-case **th**
- reading words/sentences
- identifying puzzle words and phrases
- rhyming and spelling
- reading and printing sentences from copy

Lesson 28

Consonant digraph **th**

- recognize **th** at the beginning or end of a word

- matching pictures to sentences
- printing sentences from copy
- reading "make-up" words
- puzzle words/phrases
- rhyming
- crossword puzzle with missing vowel

Lesson 29

Consonant digraph **ch**

- rule for consonant digraph **ch**
- matching pictures to sound
- using capital letters for names
- printing upper-case/lower-case **ch**
- reading sentences
- matching words/pictures
- matching puzzle words and phrases
- spelling

Lesson 30

Consonant digraph **wh**

- rule for consonant digraph **wh**
- identify capital and lower-case letters
- proper names
- identify nonsense words
- create nonsense words from sounds
- printing sentences from copy
- spelling
- use of question mark (?) and words to identify question sentences

Lesson 31

Review **th, ch, wh**

- picture/word review
- picture to sound
- printing
- auditory discrimination from word list
- spelling
- puzzle/"make-up" words and sentences
- recognizing words starting with ch within sentences

Lesson 32

Consonant digraph **sh**

- rule for beginning consonant digraph **sh**
- printing practice with capital and lower-case **sh**
- picture/word match
- puzzle/make-believe words and phrases
- word search
- printing sentences from copy
- rhyming
- spelling

Lesson 33

Consonant digraph **sh**

- rule for **sh** endings
- printing practice with and lower-case **sh**
- picture/beginning sound
- sentences to match picture
- rhyming
- alphabetize
- print sentences from copy
- identify sh at end of word

Lesson 34

Review consonant digraphs **th, ch, wh, sh**

- picture/sound identification
- printing/identifying ending sound
- word/picture identification
- auditory discrimination from word list
- spelling
- printing from copy

Lesson 35

Silent **e: ā ȩ**

- rule for silent **e: a ȩ**
- picture to sound
- diacritical marking
- short/long **a** contrast
- picture/sentence match
- puzzle/make-believe words and phrases
- spelling
- sentence completion
- word identification without pictures

Lesson 36

Consonant blend **bl**

- rule for blend **bl**
- picture to sound
- printing practice with capital and lower-case **bl**
- printing from copy
- picture to sentence match
- spelling
- word to picture match
- puzzle/make-believe words and phrases
- beginning blend choice

Lesson 37

Consonant blend **br**

- rule for blend **br**
- picture to sound
- printing practice with capital and lower-case **br**
- word identification – diacritical marking
- word/picture identification of sound
- sentence to picture match
- puzzle/make-believe words and sentences
- spelling
- sentence completion
- printing sentence from copy

Lesson 38

Consonant blend **cl**

- rule for blend **cl**
- picture to sound
- printing practice with capital and lower-case **cl**
- word/picture identification for printing
- beginning blend printing/spelling
- picture to word match
- puzzle/make-believe words and phrases
- printing sentence from copy

Lesson 39

Consonant blend **cr**

- rule for consonant blend **cr**
- picture to sound
- printing practice with capital and lower-case **cr**
- picture to word match
- printing beginning sounds
- word/picture identification for printing
- alphabetize
- sentence completion
- puzzle/make-believe words and phrases
- spelling

Lesson 40

Review consonant blends **cr**, **cl**, **br**, **bl**

- word/picture identification
- auditory discrimination from word list
- puzzle/make-believe words and phrases
- spelling – fill in beginning and ending sounds
- sentence printing from copy

Lesson 41

Silent **e**: **ī ȼ**

- rule for silent **e**: **ī ȼ**
- word/picture identification
- diacritical marking
- word/picture match
- sentence/picture match
- puzzle/make-believe words and phrases
- spelling

Lesson 42

Consonant blend **dr** – question sentences

- rule for consonant blend **dr**
- word/picture identification
- practice printing with capital and lower-case **dr**
- word/picture match
- printing beginning sounds for picture

- choice of beginning sounds
- puzzle/make-believe words and phrases
- rule for question marks and sentences
- review of question words and use of question marks
- spelling
- rhyming

Lesson 43

Consonant blend **fl**

- rule for consonant blend **fl**
- practice printing with capital and lower-case **fl**
- beginning sounds identified
- printing beginning sounds
- alphabetical order
- sentence completion
- puzzle/make-believe words and phrases
- sentence printing from copy

Lesson 44

Review silent **e**: **ā ȼ** and **ī ȼ** with single consonant beginnings

- review silent e rule
- diacritical marking
- picture/word identification
- printing – place in columns
- word/picture match
- auditory discrimination from word list
- spelling
- sentence completion

Lesson 45

Review silent **e**: **ā ȼ** and **ī ȼ** with consonant blend beginnings

- review silent **e** rule
- picture to sound – diacritical markings
- printing – place in columns
- word/picture match
- auditory discrimination from word list
- spelling
- sentence completion from pictures
- sentence completion – original

Lesson 46

Ending **ck**
- rule for **ck** ending
- picture/sound identification
- placement of sound within word
- picture/sentence match
- rhyming
- alphabetical order
- puzzle/make-believe words and phrases
- spelling

Lesson 47

Ending **ing**
- rule for **ing** ending
- picture to sound
- word identification
- picture to word match
- picture/sentence identification and printing
- word completion
- sentence completion
- printing
- auditory discrimination from word list

Lesson 48

Review short and long vowels
- short vowel identification
- long vowel identification
- word/picture match
- puzzle/make-believe words and phrases
- auditory discrimination for word list
- word comprehension from sentence
- spelling

Lesson 49

Silent **e**: **ō** **¢** – filling in sentences
- rule of silent **e**: **ō** **¢**
- word/picture identification
- printing short and long vowel words - dia-critical marking
- word ending choice from pictures
- auditory discrimination from word list

- sentence completion
- rhyming
- puzzle and make believe words
- printing from copy

Lesson 50

Consonant blend **gr**
- rule for consonant blend **gr**
- word/picture match
- practice printing capital and lower case **gr**
- beginning sound identification
- word/picture match
- printing (spelling) beginning sounds from picture
- alphabetical order
- sentence completion
- puzzle/make-believe words and phrases
- word search

Lesson 51

Consonant blend **gl**
- rule for consonant blend **gl**
- word/picture match
- practice printing capital and lower case **gl**
- beginning sound identification
- alphabetical order
- ending sound identification
- auditory discrimination from word list
- sentence completion
- printing sentence from copy

Lesson 52

Consonant blend **sp** – beginning and ending
- rule for consonant blend **sp**
- word/picture match – beginning **sp**
- practice printing **sp** with capital
- word/picture match – ending **sp**
- sentence/picture match
- puzzle/make-believe words and phrases
- spelling and rhyming
- printing sentence from copy

Lesson 53

Consonant digraph ending **tch** and **ch**

- rule for consonant digraph **tch** and **ch**
- word/picture identification of sound
- word/picture match
- discrimination of **ch** and **tch**
- puzzle/make-believe words and phrases
- spelling
- auditory discrimination from word list
- crossword puzzle
- sentence printing from copy

Lesson 54

Review short vowels and silent **e**: ā ¢, ī ¢, ō ¢

- vowel identification
- diacritical marking
- change words from short to long vowel sounds
- words in columns – long **o**, **i**, **a**
- word/picture match
- word/sentence match
- rhyming

Lesson 55

Silent **e**: ū ¢

- review silent **e** rule
- word/picture identification
- print words to match pictures – copy
- sentence completion
- puzzle/make-believe words and phrases
- spelling
- separate columns for long vowel sounds
- auditory discrimination from word list

Lesson 56

Review short and long vowels with blends

- word/picture identification
- beginning or end sound identification
- sentence completion
- rhyming
- printing question sentence from copy

Lesson 57

Review short and long vowels with consonant single and blend beginning

- beginning sound identification/word/ picture
- sentence completion
- printing sentence from copy

Lesson 58

Consonant endings **nd**, **nt** – nouns

- rule for consonant endings **nd**, **nt**
- word/picture identification
- printing
- consonant ending discrimination
- auditory discrimination from word list
- rule for nouns – person, thing
- noun identification
- noun recognition of name from sentences
- noun recognition of place from sentences
- word/picture comprehension choice

Lesson 59

Consonant ending **ng** – noun review

- word/picture identification
- printing
- ending sound identification from pictures
- auditory discrimination from word list
- noun identification
- sentence/picture comprehension choice
- rhyming
- printing sentence from copy

Lesson 60

Consonant ending **nk** – writing question sentences

- rule for consonant ending **nk**
- word/picture identification
- printing
- ending discrimination
- auditory discrimination from word list
- sentence completion
- rhyming

- yes/no to question sentences
- printing choice of question sentence

Lesson 61

Review consonant blends **ng**, **nk**, **nd**, **nt**
- word endings identification
- auditory discrimination from word list
- noun identification
- printing
- spelling
- alphabetical order

Lesson 62

Consonant blends **sc** and **sk** beginnings
- rule for consonant blends **sc** and **sk**
- word/picture identification – **sc**
- printing
- word/picture identification – **sk**
- auditory discrimination from word list
- picture/sentence comprehension
- nouns – sentence identification
- sentence comprehension, completion and identification from picture

Lesson 63

Consonant blend **sk** endings
- rule for consonant blend **sk** ending
- work/picture identification
- printing
- word/picture match
- auditory discrimination from word list
- rhyming
- word/picture identification
- spelling
- sentence/picture comprehension
- alphabetical order

Lesson 64

Consonant blend **mp** endings – sentences
- rule for consonant blend **mp** endings
- picture/word identification
- printing
- word/picture discrimination
- auditory discrimination

- rhyming
- rule for description of sentence structure
- exclamation sentences
- question sentences
- statement sentences
- printing choice of sentences from copy

Lesson 65

Consonant ending **lp** – question sentences
- picture/word association
- printing
- picture/word discrimination
- printing choice from pictures – punctuation – question mark – period
- introduction to action words
- writing from copy with choice of action words
- spelling
- auditory discrimination from word list

Lesson 66

Consonant ending **lk** – vocabulary
- rule for consonant ending **lk**
- picture/word discrimination
- spelling choice for sentence completion and comprehension
- auditory discrimination from word list
- word/picture match
- spelling – ending sounds
- picture/sentence comprehension
- printing sentences from copy – punctuation

Lesson 67

Review endings **sk**, **mp**, **lp**, **lk** with short vowels
- picture/ending sound identification
- printing
- spelling
- auditory discrimination from word list
- sentence completion
- alphabetical order

Lesson 68

Review consonant blends
- word/picture identification
- beginning or ending sound discrimination
- spelling
- alphabetical order
- sentence completion
- rhyming
- writing sentence from copy

Lesson 69

Beginning consonant blend **pl** – pronouns
- rule for consonant blend **pl**
- word/picture identification
- practice printing **pl** with capital and lower-case letters
- picture/word beginning sound identification
- picture/word match
- alphabetical order
- Review noun rule
- rule – pronoun
- read sentences – change from noun to pronoun
- write sentence from copy – identify pronoun

Lesson 70

Review beginning consonant blends
- picture/beginning sound identification
- printing
- noun identification
- pronoun identification
- creative sentence making

Lesson 71

Double vowels – **ai**
- rule for double vowels – **ai**
- picture/sound identification
- word/picture match
- print rhyming words from copy
- puzzle/make-believe words and phrases
- sentence completion

- spelling
- printing sentence from copy

Lesson 72

Consonant blends with **ai**
- picture/sound identification
- printing
- puzzle/make-believe words and phrases
- picture/word and sound discrimination
- sentence/picture match
- sentence completion
- alphabetical order

Lesson 73

Consonant blend beginnings **pr**, **tr** – quotation marks
- rule for consonant blend beginnings **pr** and **tr**
- picture/word sound discrimination
- printing
- pictures/choice of beginning sounds
- word/picture match
- rule for quotation marks.
- read sentences
- print sentences using quotation marks

Lesson 74

Consonant blend beginning **sl**
- rule for consonant blend **sl**
- picture/word sound discrimination
- practice printing letters – capital and lower-case
- picture/beginning sound association
- picture/word match
- spelling
- puzzle/make-believe words and phrases
- create puzzle words

Lesson 75

Consonant blend beginning **sm**
- rule for consonant blend **sm**
- picture/word sound discrimination

- practice printing letters – capital and lower-case
- word/picture match
- sentence/picture match
- rhyming
- quotation marks
- spelling
- alphabetical order

Lesson 76

Consonant blend **sn**

- rule for consonant blend **sn**
- picture/word sound discrimination
- practice printing letters – capital and lower-case
- word/picture match
- sentence/picture match
- rhyming
- picture/sentence comprehension
- auditory discrimination from word list

Lesson 77

Review of consonant blends and digraphs

- pictures/sound discrimination
- auditory discrimination from word list
- auditory discrimination identifying ending sounds

Lesson 78

Double vowels – **ea**

- rule for double vowels **ea**
- picture/sound identification
- picture – printing and diacritical marking
- picture/word match
- puzzle/make-believe words and phrases
- rhyming
- sentence completion
- spelling
- printing sentence from copy

Lesson 79

Double vowels – **ee**

- rule for double vowels **ee**
- picture/sound identification

- picture – printing and diacritical marking
- picture/word match
- rhyming
- puzzle/make-believe words and phrases
- sentence/picture match
- spelling
- printing sentence from copy

Lesson 80

Beginning **qu** – picture sequence

- rule for **qu**
- picture/sound identification
- practice printing with capital and lower-case
- picture/word match
- rhyming
- sentence/picture match
- picture sequence

Lesson 81

Beginning blend **scr** – picture sequence

- picture/sound identification
- practice printing with capital and lower-case
- picture/word match
- printing sentence from copy – quotation marks
- spelling
- sentence sequence
- yes/no questions

Lesson 82

Review of double vowels – beginning blends

- picture/sound identification
- auditory discrimination from word list
- spelling
- picture/sentence comprehension
- sentence completion

Lesson 83

Double vowels – **oa**

- review double vowel rule – include **oa**
- picture/sound identification
- printing – diacritical marking

- word/picture match
- rhyming
- puzzle/make-believe words and phrases
- sentence comprehension/pictures
- spelling
- printing sentence from copy

Lesson 84

Beginning blend **fr**

- rule for beginning blend **fr**
- picture/sound identification
- practice printing with capital and lower-case
- picture/word match
- rhyming
- puzzle/make-believe words and phrases
- printing for sentence completion
- spelling
- yes/no sentence
- printing sentence from copy

Lesson 85

Consonant endings **lt**, **lf**

- rule for consonant ending **lt** and **lf**
- picture/sound identification
- reading – sentence comprehension
- auditory discrimination
- spelling
- printing – punctuation
- picture/sentence match

Lesson 86

Consonant ending **ft** – following directions

- rule for consonant ending **ft**
- picture/sound identification
- printing
- word ending sound identification
- auditory discrimination from word list
- picture/sentence comprehension
- follow directions
- word/picture match

Lesson 87

Review consonant endings

- pictures/sound identification
- sentence completion
- rhyme/picture
- auditory discrimination from word list
- spelling

Lesson 88

Review long and short vowel sounds

- picture/sound identification
- change word from short to long – diacritical marking
- column choice for words
- sentence completion

Lesson 89

Consonant blend beginnings **spr**, **spl**

- rule for consonant blend beginnings **spr**, **spl**
- picture/sound identification
- practice printing with capital and lower-case
- picture/sound discrimination
- word to word match
- read sentences from copy – print quotation marks
- alphabetical order
- sentence sequence for story

Lesson 90

Consonant blend beginning **st**

- rule for consonant blend beginning **st**
- picture/sound identification
- practice printing with capital and lower-case
- picture/word match
- rhyming
- puzzle/make-believe words and phrases
- sentence completion
- yes/no choice
- spelling

Lesson 91

Consonant blend review – **tch**, **sp**, **ft**

- ending sound identification
- printing
- picture/sentence comprehension match
- read sentences – vocabulary comprehension
- rhyming
- yes/no choice
- printing sentence from copy

Lesson 92

Consonant blend ending **st**

- rule for consonant blend ending **st**
- printing
- picture/sound identification
- auditory discrimination from word list
- rhyming
- reading sentences – vocabulary enrichment
- spelling
- sentence completion

Lesson 93

Review consonant endings – **tch**, **sp**, **st**, **lt**, **lf**, **ft**

- picture/sound identification
- auditory discrimination from word list
- sentence completion
- rhyming
- spelling – end sounds
- sentence choice to match picture

Lesson 94

Consonant blends **tw**, **sw**

- picture/sound identification
- puzzle/make-believe words and sentences
- printing sentence from copy
- sentence completion
- yes/no choice
- spelling

Lesson 95

Review consonant beginnings **tw**, **sp**, **st**, **spl**, **spr**, **qu**

- picture/sound identification
- auditory discrimination from word list
- sentence completion
- rhyming
- spelling
- yes/no choice
- alphabetical order
- print sentences – quotation marks

Lesson 96

Review endings **lf**, **ft**, **ng**, **nk**, **lk**, **lp**, **sk**, **sh**

- picture/sound discrimination
- sentence completion
- alphabetical order
- spelling
- could be/no way
- columns for endings
- read sentences – vocabulary development

Lesson 97

Vowel plus **r: ar**

- rule for vowel plus **r: ar**
- picture/sound identification
- practice printing with lower-case
- sentence/picture match – **ar** recognition
- rhyming
- puzzle/make-believe words and phrases
- read sentences – vocabulary development
- word search

Lesson 98

Vowel plus **r: or**

- rule for vowel plus **r: or**
- picture/sound identification
- practice printing with lower-case
- sentence/picture match – **or** recognition
- puzzle/make-believe words and phrases
- read sentences – vocabulary development
- sentence completion
- printing sentences – capitals/punctuation

Lesson 99

Review vowel plus **r**: **ar**, **or**

- picture/sound identification
- practice printing
- sentence completion
- alphabetical order
- spelling
- could be/no way
- read sentences – vocabulary development
- auditory discrimination from word list

Lesson 100

Review vowel plus **r**: **ar**

- picture/sound identification
- spelling
- sentence completion
- sentence/picture match – identify **ar**
- puzzle/make-believe words and phrases
- auditory discrimination from word list
- read sentences – vocabulary development

Lesson 101

Review vowel plus **r**: **or**

- picture/sound identification
- spelling
- sentence completion
- alphabetical order
- yes/no choice
- read sentences – vocabulary development
- crossword puzzle

Lesson 102

Vowel plus **r**: **er**, **ir**, **ur**

- rule for vowel plus **r**: **er**, **ir**, **ur**
- sound identification from written word
- printing
- picture/sentence match – **er** sound identification
- puzzle/make-believe words and phrases
- read sentences – vocabulary development
- could be/no way

Lesson 103

Vowel plus **r**: **ir**

- review rule for vowel plus **r**: **ir**
- sound identification from written word
- printing
- picture/sentence match – **ir** sound identification
- puzzle/make-believe words and phrases
- read sentences – vocabulary development
- auditory discrimination

Lesson 104

Vowel plus **r**: **ur**

- review rule for vowel plus **r**: **ur**
- printing
- picture/sentence match – **ur** sound identification
- puzzle/make-believe words and phrases
- read sentences – vocabulary development
- sound identification

Lesson 105

Review vowel plus **r**: **er**, **ir**, **ur**

- picture/sound association
- sentence completion
- printing
- sentence/picture match – sound identification
- words in column
- rhyming
- auditory discrimination from word list
- could be/no way

Lesson 106

Review vowel plus **r**: **ar**, **or**

- picture/sound association
- sentence completion
- alphabetical order
- picture/sentence match
- words in columns
- yes/no
- rhyming

Lesson 107

Review all vowels plus **r**

- picture/sound association
- sentence completion
- alphabetical order
- rhyming
- picture/sentence match
- word/picture match

Lesson 108

Plurals – **s**

- rule for plurals – **s**
- singular and plural identification
- spelling
- picture/phrase match
- sentence completion
- pictures – choice of plurals or singular

Lesson 109

Plurals – **es**

- rule for plurals – **es**
- spelling
- picture/phrase match
- sentence completion
- pictures – choice of plurals or singular

Lesson 110

Plurals – **y** into **ies**

- rule for **y** into **ies**
- spelling
- picture – plural identification
- phrase/picture match
- sentence completion
- pictures – choice of plurals or singular

Lesson 111

Review plurals – **s**, **es**, **ies**

- plural identification
- spelling
- word identification with plurals
- sentence/picture match – identify plurals

Lesson 112

Review double vowels – **ee**

- review rule for double vowels – **ee**
- picture/sound identification
- print/diacritical markings
- word/picture match
- rhyming
- puzzle/make-believe words and phrases
- sentence comprehension
- spelling
- alphabetical order

Lesson 113

Review double vowels – **ee**, **oa** – apostrophe

- picture/sound association
- printing – diacritical markings
- sentence completion
- spelling
- rhyming
- rule for apostrophe – possession
- sentence exchange – single possession
- sentence exchange – plural possession

Lesson 114

Review double vowels – **ai**, **ea**

- picture/sound association
- column printing
- sentence completion
- spelling
- review apostrophe rule
- sentence exchange – single possession
- sentence exchange – plural possession

Lesson 115

Review all double vowels

- picture/sound association
- printing – diacritical markings
- sentence completion
- puzzle/make-believe words and phrases
- spelling

Lesson 116

Digraph **ay**

- rule for digraph **ay**
- picture/sound association
- printing
- rhyming
- puzzle/make-believe words and phrases
- sentence comprehension
- spelling
- alphabetical order

Lesson 117

Digraph **ey**

- rule for digraph **ey**
- picture/sound association
- printing – diacritical marking
- read sentences – vocabulary development
- rhyming
- puzzle/make-believe words and phrases
- alphabetical order

Lesson 118

Review digraphs **ay**, **ey** – apostrophe

- review digraph rule – **ay**, **ey**
- word/sound association
- sentence completion
- picture/word match
- spelling
- review apostrophe rule
- print sentence exchange for single possession
- print sentence exchange for plural possession

Lesson 119

Diphthong **ow**

- rule for diphthong **ow**
- word/sound association
- picture/word match
- sentence completion
- auditory determination from word list
- printing from copy

Lesson 120

Diphthong **ou**

- rule for both sounds of **ou**
- picture/sound association
- sentence completion
- printing sentences from copy – identify punctuation

Lesson 121

Review digraphs **ay**, **ey**

- picture/sound association
- word/picture match
- spelling
- sentence completion
- noun identification
- sentence sequence
- alphabetical order
- picture/sentence match – **ay**, **ey** identified
- auditory discrimination from word list
- make-believe sentences

Lesson 122

Review digraphs **ay**, **ey**; diphthongs **ow**, **ou**

- picture/word association
- spelling
- sentence completion
- word/picture match – sound identification
- auditory discrimination from word bank
- make-believe phrase

Lesson 123

Digraphs **aw**, **au** – proper nouns – creative writing

- rule for digraphs **aw**, **au**
- picture/sound association
- picture/word match
- word/sound association
- spelling
- sentence completion
- printing – punctuation
- creative writing

- sentence printing – proper nouns
- make-believe phrase

Lesson 124

Digraph **ew**

- rule for digraph **ew**
- picture/sound association
- picture/word match
- spelling
- sentence completion
- review proper nouns
- rule for common noun
- common nouns in sentences
- printing sentences – quotation marks
- auditory discrimination
- make-believe phrase

Lesson 125

Diphthong **oy**

- rule for diphthong **oy**
- picture/sound association
- spelling
- word/picture match
- sentence completion
- proper and common noun identification
- quotation marks
- alphabetical order
- printing
- auditory discrimination from word list

Lesson 126

Review digraphs **aw**, **au**, **ew**; diphthong **oy**

- picture/sound association
- picture/word match
- auditory discrimination from word list
- sentence completion
- printing
- rhyming

Lesson 127

Diphthong **oi**

- rule for diphthong **oi**
- picture/sound association
- picture/word match

- printing
- sentences – sound identification
- make-believe phrases
- spelling
- sentences – vocabulary development
- printing – punctuation

Lesson 128

Review diphthongs **ow**, **ou**; digraphs **ay**, **ey**

- picture/sound association
- sentence completion
- alphabetical order
- rhyming
- sentence/picture match
- printing – punctuation
- auditory discrimination from word list

Lesson 129

Review digraphs **aw**, **au**, **ew**

- picture/sound association
- sentence completion
- picture/word match
- sentences – quotation marks
- auditory discrimination from word list
- spelling
- make-believe phrases

Lesson 130

Review **ow**, **ou**

- picture/sound association
- picture/word match
- spelling
- sentences – sound discrimination
- make-believe phrase
- sentences – punctuation
- auditory discrimination from word list

Lesson 131

Review diphthongs **oy**, **oi**

- picture/sound association
- picture/word match
- spelling
- auditory discrimination from word list
- sentences – sound discrimination

- sentence/picture match
- rhyming
- printing/punctuation

Lesson 132

Letter **y** as in **cry**
- rule for letter **y** as in **cry**
- picture/sound association
- spelling
- word/picture match
- read sentences – vocabulary development
- rhyming
- sentence completion
- auditory discrimination from word list
- printing

Lesson 133

Letter **y** as in **baby**
- rule for Letter **y** as in **baby**
- picture/sound association
- spelling
- word/picture match
- read sentences – vocabulary development
- rhyming
- sentence completion
- auditory discrimination from word list
- printing sentence

Lesson 134

Review Letter **y** as in **cry**, **baby**
- review letter **y** sounds
- picture/sound association
- column printing
- sentence completion
- capitalization – proper nouns
- spelling
- auditory discrimination from word list

Lesson 135

Vowel digraph – special **oo** as in **book**
- rule for vowel digraph – **oo** as in **book**
- picture/printing

- read sentences/sound association
- printing
- auditory discrimination from word list
- rhyming
- read sentences – vocabulary development

Lesson 136

Vowel digraph – special **oo** as in **tooth**
- Rule for vowel digraph – special **oo** as in **tooth**
- picture/printing
- read sentences/sound association
- printing
- auditory discrimination from word list
- rhyming
- read sentences – vocabulary development
- printing sentence from copy

Lesson 137

Review all digraphs/diphthongs
- spelling
- sentence/picture match
- common nouns

Lesson 138

Review letter **y** – long **i** and **e**
- spelling
- sentence completion
- rhyming
- auditory discrimination from word list

Lesson 139

Silent letter **w**
- rule for silent **w**
- picture/word association
- spelling
- printing
- sentences/word identification
- auditory discrimination from word list
- picture description
- make-believe phrase

Lesson 140

Silent letter **k**

- rule for silent **k**
- picture/word association
- spelling
- printing
- make-believe phrase
- auditory discrimination
- sentences – word identification
- picture description

Lesson 141

Silent letter **b**

- rule for silent **b**
- picture/word association
- spelling
- printing
- make-believe phrase
- auditory discrimination from word list
- sentences – word identification
- word discrimination

Lesson 142

Review silent letters **b**, **k**, **w**

- word identification
- word/picture match
- spelling
- auditory discrimination from word list
- sentence/picture match
- identify silent letters
- letter writing

Lesson 143

Silent letter **g**

- rule for silent **g**
- printing
- spelling
- word discrimination
- sentence/picture match
- auditory discrimination from word list
- spelling
- picture description
- questions

Lesson 144

Silent **gh**

- rule for silent **gh**
- word/picture association
- spelling
- phrase match
- auditory discrimination from word list
- sentence/picture match
- puzzle picture

Lesson 145

Review silent letters – **w**, **k**, **b**, **gn**, **gh**

- word/picture identification
- column printing
- auditory discrimination from word list
- word identification
- story comprehension
- creative sentence writing

Lesson 146

le endings

- rule for words ending in le
- word/picture identification
- printing
- word/picture match
- sentence/word identification
- make-believe phrase
- sentence completion
- story comprehension

Lesson 147

Words with **all**

- rule for words with **all**
- word/picture association
- printing
- word/picture match
- spelling
- sentence/word identification
- make-believe phrases
- sentence/comprehension
- story comprehension
- creative sentence writing

Lesson 148

Syllables – double consonants
- rule for double consonants
- word/picture identification
- printing
- sentence/word discrimination

Lesson 149

Syllables – compound words
- rule for syllables with compound words
- word/picture identification
- printing compound words
- word-parts match
- sentences word identification
- make-believe phrase
- word identification
- compound word identification

Lesson 150

Syllables – consonant between vowels
- rule for syllables
- syllable recognition
- printing
- sentences/syllable recognition
- auditory discrimination from word list
- make-believe phrases
- sentences – punctuation
- picture sequence

Lesson 151

Review syllables
- compound word identification
- word/picture match
- sentence completion
- creative sentences using compound words
- creative sentences using double consonants

Lesson 152

Suffix **ing** – prepositions
- signal for word ending with ing
- word/picture match
- spelling
- sentence completion – base word
- rule for prepositions
- picture/identify prepositional phrases

Lesson 153

Special soft **c**
- rule for soft **c**
- reading/printing
- word/picture match
- spelling
- sentences/word identification
- sentence completion
- review noun rule
- identify nouns in sentences
- creative writing of nouns

Lesson 154

Special soft **g**
- rule for soft **g**
- reading/printing
- word/picture match
- spelling
- column printing
- alphabetical order
- make-believe phrases
- sentences/word identification
- picture sequence

Lesson 155

Review ending **ing**, soft **c**, soft **g**
- base word completion
- sentence completion
- picture/word choice
- sentence completion
- sentence sequence
- creative sentence

Lesson 156

Non-phonetic **alk**, **ph** – contractions
- rule for **ph**
- picture/word identification
- printing
- word/picture match

- spelling
- sentence completion
- rule for words with **alk**
- picture/word
- read sentences/vocabulary development
- rule for contractions
- words for contractions
- creative use of contractions

Lesson 157

Non-phonetic **old**, **ost**, **olt**

- rule for non-phonetic word parts – **old**, **ost**, **olt**
- picture/word identification
- printing
- word/picture match
- read sentences/vocabulary development
- action verbs
- sentence completion
- sentence/picture match – action verb identified
- creative action verb

Lesson 158

Non-phonetic **ild**, **ind**

- rule for non-phonetic word parts – **ild**, **ind**
- picture/word identification
- printing
- spelling
- sentence completion
- nouns: proper, common
- pronouns
- verbs
- creative sentences

Lesson 159

Review non-phonetic word parts – **alk**, **old**, **ost**, **olt**, **ind**, **ild**

- picture/word match
- printing
- spelling
- picture/word completion choice
- sentence completion
- crossword puzzle
- auditory discrimination

Lesson 160

Review all

- spelling
- plurals
- double vowels
- silent **e**
- picture/word match
- diacritical markings
- double consonants
- syllables
- compound words
- soft **c** and **g**
- picture/word match

Teacher's Lessons

Lesson 121 - Review: Digraphs ay, ey; Common Nouns

Overview:

- Digraphs **ay**, **ey**
- Sentence completion
- Picture sequencing
- Common nouns

Materials and Supplies:

- Teacher's Guide & Student Workbook
- White board
- Reader 4: *Van's Scarecrow*

Teaching Tips:

Review digraphs **ay**, **ey** using the white board as necessary. Discuss all the pictures in each activity so the student is able to identify them.

Introduce common nouns by naming objects or pictures of things in the room.

Activity 1. Review names of pictures together. Have the student put a CIRCLE around the pictures that have the sound of **ay** as in **pay**.

Pictures: **hay, honey, tray, x-ray, pray, jay, gray, key**

Activity 2. Put a SQUARE around the pictures that have the sound of **ey** as in **key**.

Pictures: **donkey, monkey, train, key honey, scarf, clay, money**

Activity 3. Read the words together. Have the student draw a line from the word to the picture it matches.

Pictures: **tray, pray, monkey, honey, money**

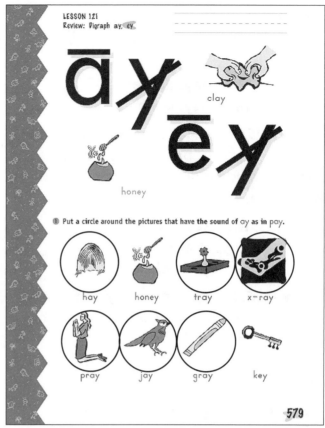

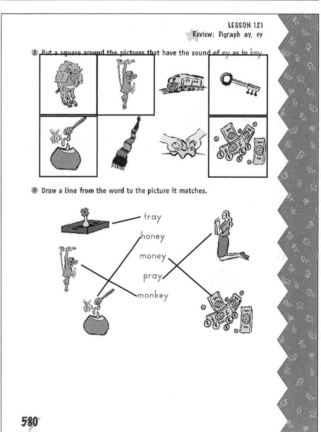

Activity 4. Spell the following words by adding the digraph **ay** or **ey** under the picture.

> Pictures: tr**ay**, p**ay**, donk**ey**
>
> h**ay**, cl**ay**, k**ey**

Activity 5. Introduce common nouns by naming objects or pictures in the room . Have the student draw a line from the common nouns to the picture it matches.

> Pictures: **monkey, wheel,**
>
> **key, chain,**
>
> **honey, donkey**

Activity 6. Read the sentences and words together. Have the student choose the correct word to complete the sentence.

1. We go to church and (**pray**) each Sunday.
2. Fay put the (**tray**) on the desk.
3. A (**donkey**) lives in the barn.
4. The (**key**) does not fit in the lock.
5. We saw the bees make (**honey**).
6. Our dog will (**stray**) if we do not tie him to his house.

Activity 7. Discuss the pictures together, noting the sequence. Have the student put **1** under the one that happens first; **2** under the next one; and **3** under the one that would happen last.

1. **Boy pays his way into the zoo.**
2. **Boy looks for monkeys.**
3. **Boy feeds monkey.**

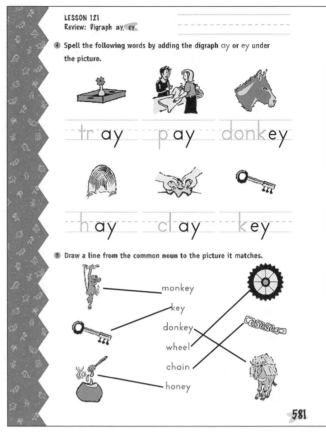

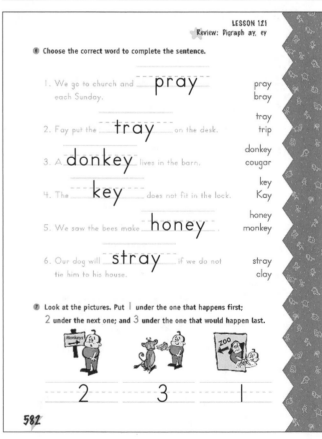

Horizons Kindergarten Phonics

Activity 8. Put the words in alphabetical order.

Words: **chair, dock, frog, monkey**

Activity 9. Read the sentences together. Have the student draw a line from the picture to match the sentence. Underline all the words with **ay** or **ey** in them.

Pictures: **The jay in our tree is making a nest.**
Mike lost the key to his trunk.
They cut the hay for the cows to eat.
There is a big monkey at the zoo.

Activity 10. Read one word from each line and have the student put a circle around the correct word in that line.

1. **stay, stem, stick**
2. **monkey, money, Mike**
3. **donkey, dust, day**
4. **pray, pick, pack**

Activity 11. Draw a line from the puzzle sentence to the picture it matches.

Pictures: **The monkey can sit on money.**
The donkey can pray at the church.
There is rust in the honey.
A dog was sitting in a clay pot.

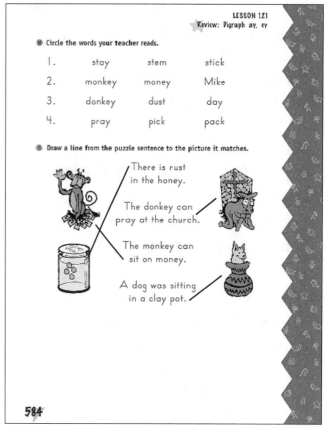

Lesson 122 - Review: Digraphs ay, ey; Diphthongs ow, ou

Overview:

- Digraphs **ay, ey** and diphthongs **ow, ou**
- Sentence completion
- Auditory discrimination

Materials and Supplies:

- Teacher's Guide & Student Workbook
- White board
- Reader 4: *Jays*

Teaching Tips:

Review all the pictures in each activity to be sure the student is able to identify them.

Review the digraphs **ay, ey** and diphthongs **ow, ou,** using the white board as necessary.

Activity 1. Be sure the student can identify the pictures. Have him put a CIRCLE around the pictures that have the **ay** sound. Put a SQUARE around the pictures that have the **ey** sound.

Pictures: **donkey, play, monkey, tray
key, pray, money, hockey**

Activity 2. Draw a line from the picture to the word it matches.

Pictures: **money, donkey, valley, key, play, pay**

Activity 3. Spell the following words by adding **ay, ey, ow,** or **ou** under the pictures.

Pictures: rainb**ow**, cl**ay**, shad**ow**
pill**ow**, gr**ay**, hock**ey**
mon**ey**, k**ey**, tr**ay**

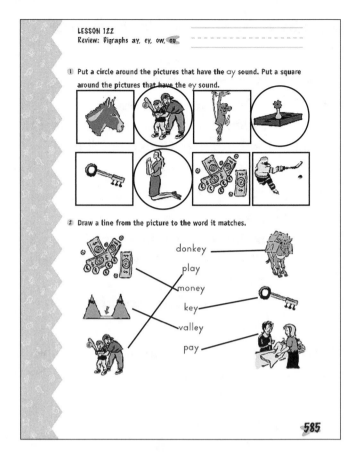

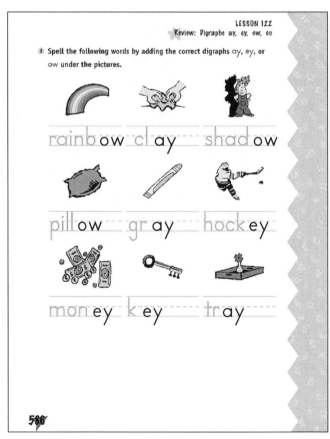

Activity 4. Read the sentences together. Have the student choose and print the correct word from the word bank to complete the sentences.

1. The (**elbow**) of my left arm is weak.
2. Bill rode the (**donkey**) into town.
3. There is a (**key**) for the lock of my trunk.
4. Brad keeps his (**money**) in a big bank.

Activity 5. Rewrite the sentence using capitalization and punctuation.

[**I**]t is time to go to the show[**.**]

Activity 6. Read the sentences together and discuss the pictures. Have the student draw a line from the picture to match the sentence. Underline all the words that have **ey** or **ay** in them.

Pictures: **How much money did you pay for the car?**
Do you have the key in your hand?
The donkey has long ears.

Activity 7. Read one word from each of the boxes and have the student put a circle around the correct word in each box.

Words: **stay, money, clay,**
pray, pack, punk,
key, may, brake,
hay, play, tray

Activity 8. Draw a line from the puzzle phrase to the picture it matches.

Pictures: **a tray with hay**
a jay on a tray
a key on a donkey
a monkey with money

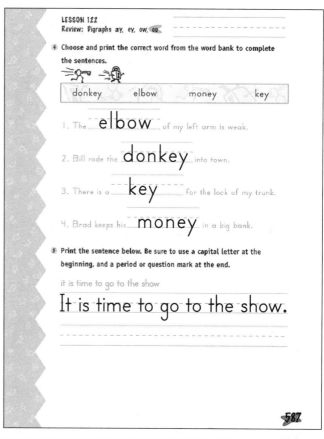

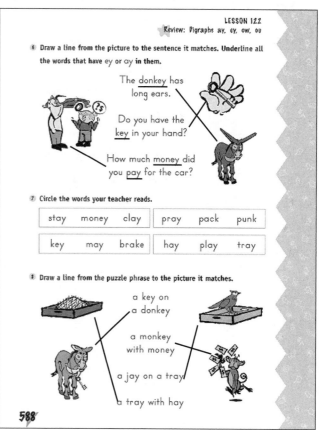

Horizons Kindergarten Phonics

31

Lesson 123 - Digraphs aw, au; Proper Nouns

Overview:

- Digraphs **aw** and **au**
- Spelling
- Sentence completion
- Proper nouns

Materials and Supplies:

- Teacher's Guide & Student Workbook
- White board
- Reader 4: *The Dump Truck*

Teaching Tips:

Use the white board to introduce the digraphs **aw** and **au** as the vowels are blended in the words **saw** and **Paul**.

Teach proper nouns by using the student's own name and names of family or friends. In addition, show the proper noun use in cities, states, and titles of books, etc.

Activity 1. Discuss each picture, the sound, and its meanings. Have the student put a circle around the pictures that have the sound we hear in the words **saw** and **Paul**.

Pictures: **spoon, claw, jaw, haul draw, shawl, hawk, auto**

LESSON 123
Digraph aw, au

aw
au

prawn

vault

In pronouncing the digraphs aw and au, the vowel sounds are blended as in saw and Paul.

① Put a circle around the pictures that have the sound we hear in the words saw and Paul.

spoon   claw   jaw   haul

draw   shawl   hawk   auto

589

Activity 2. Read the words together. Have the student draw a line from the picture to the word it matches.

Pictures: **vault, sprawl, shawl, auto, draw, lawn**

Activity 3. Look at the words under the pictures. Put a CIRCLE around the words that are spelled with **aw**. UNDERLINE the words that are spelled with **au**.

Pictures: dr**aw**, f**aw**n, P**au**l, f**au**lt, h**au**l, s**au**nter, p**aw**, l**aw**n

Activity 4. Spell the words below the pictures by putting **aw** to complete the word.

Words: h**aw**k, y**aw**n, j**aw**, cl**aw**, cr**aw**l, dr**aw**

Activity 5. Spell the words below the pictures by putting **au** to complete the word.

Words: h**au**l, v**au**lt, P**au**l, s**au**na

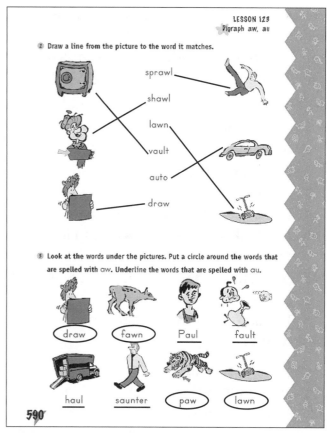

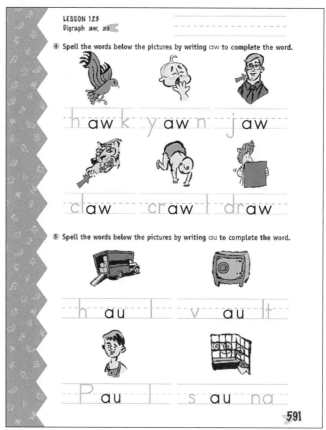

Activity 6. Read the sentences and the words in the word bank together. Discuss the meaning of each word. Have the student choose the correct word from the word bank to complete the sentence. Print it on the line.

1. Paul fell and hurt his (**jaw**).
2. We got out of bed at (**dawn**).
3. We can catch a (**prawn**) and some fish in the sea.
4. The bird let out a loud (**squawk**).
5. We think it was a (**hawk**) flying in the air.
6. Dad had to (**haul**) some dirt for his yard.
7. Jim sat in a hot (**sauna**).
8. The auto crash was not the man's (**fault**).

Activity 7. Introduce the proper noun rule. A proper noun is the name of a person or place, such as **Jack Smith** or **New York**. It must begin with a capital letter.

Activity 8. Read the sentences together and discuss the proper nouns in each sentence. Have the student print the sentence correctly by putting a capital letter on each persons name in the sentence.

> It is fun to play with **Jane** and **Fred**.
> My best friend is **Paul**.
> This boy lives in the state of **Maine**.
> We call the dog **Spot**.

Activity 9. Have your teacher help you spell the name of your town or city.

Activity 10. Have your teacher help you spell the name of your state.

Activity 11. Draw a line from the puzzle phrase to the picture it matches.

> Pictures: **a vault with a shawl**
> **a hawk that can draw**
> **haul a truck with a claw**
> **a fawn who can sprawl**

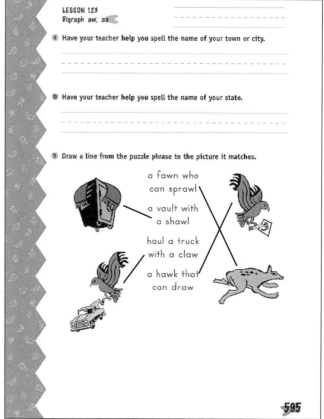

Activity 12. Draw a picture of something in this lesson. Write a sentence about your picture on the lines below.

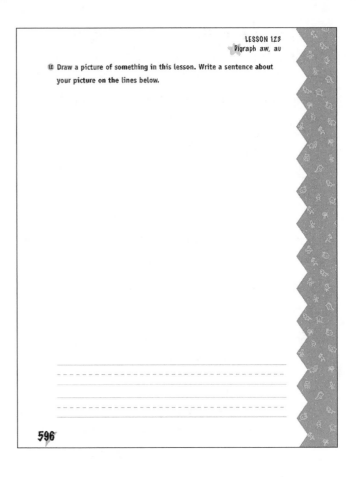

12 Draw a picture of something in this lesson. Write a sentence about your picture on the lines below.

596

Lesson 124 - Digraph ew;
Quotation Marks;
Sentences

Overview:

- Digraph **ew**
- Sentence completion
- Review common and proper nouns
- Introduce quotation marks in sentences

Materials & Supplies:

- Teacher's Guide & Student Workbook
- White board
- Reader 4: *The New Stew*

Teaching Tips:

Use the white board to introduce digraph **ew** as in **few**.

In teaching quotation, again use the white board to print exactly what is said in a contrived conversation to indicate the use of quotation marks.

Activity 1. Study the pictures and discuss the words. Have the student put a circle around the words that have the sound of **ew** as in the word **blew**.

Pictures: **threw, screw, drew, crew, blew, stew, troop, few**

Activity 2. Study the pictures and words together. Have the student draw a line from the picture to the word it matches.

Pictures: **blew, stew, threw, flew, chew, grew**

Activity 3. Spell the words below the pictures by putting **ew** to complete the word.

Pictures: f**ew**, st**ew**, thr**ew**
dr**ew**, fl**ew**, ch**ew**

Activity 4. Read the words and sentences together. Have the student choose the correct word from the word bank to complete the sentence.

1. Mom made some good (**stew**) for dinner.
2. Watch the dog (**chew**) on his bone.
3. The storm was so bad the wind (**blew**) the roof off the house.
4. Paul (**threw**) the ball over the barn.
5. Dad had to put a (**screw**) in the gate to fix it.
6. The grass (**grew**) tall in the valley.

Activity 5. Review common and proper nouns. Read the sentences together and have the student draw a line under all the proper nouns.

1. **Jan** and **Bob** went to the store.
2. When we were in town, we saw **Mr. Smith**.
3. **Jack** blew the balloon so big it burst.
4. When do you want **Drew** to come to your house?

Activity 6. Read the sentences together. Have the student put a circle around the common nouns.

1. The **cat** and **dog** can run in the **park**.
2. Where did you see the **mouse** go?
3. The **shack** is in the back **yard**.
4. Will the **tent** stand up when the **wind** blows so hard?

Activity 7. Read one word from each of the rows and have the student put a circle around the correct word.

Words: **new, raw, time**
bawl, few, fault,
threw, vault, three
cow, chew, crew

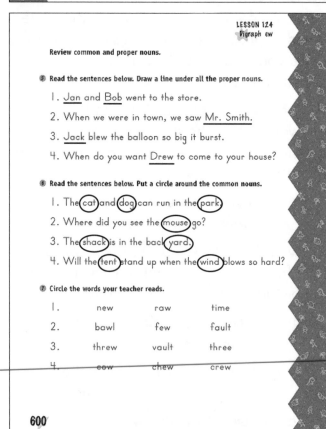

Activity 8. Introduce quotation marks around the words a person speaks. Practice conversations and identify the person speaking, and the exact words spoken. Read the sentences together and discuss the conversations. Have the student print the sentences below. Use quotation marks around the words a person speaks.

1. Frank said, ["]I like to ride horses."
2. ["]Did you like the pie?["] asked Mom.
3. ["]Yes, the pie was good,["] answered Bill.
4. ["]I want to go to school,["] said Dirk.

Activity 9. Draw a line from the puzzle phrase to the picture.

Pictures: **a dog in the hot stew**
a new hat for the feet
a cat with a big jaw
a crew of men in a tree

Activity 10. Color the picture.

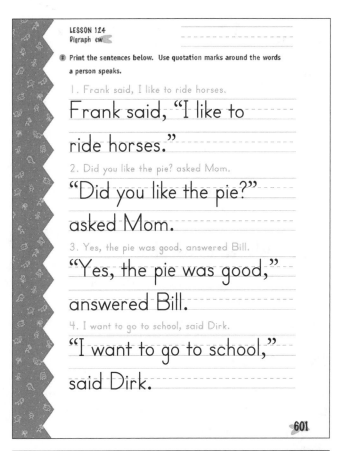

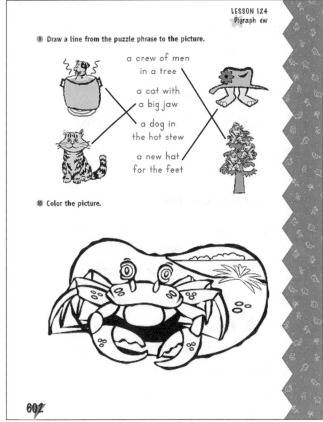

Lesson 125 - Diphthong oy

Overview:

- Diphthong **oy**
- Spelling
- Sentence completion
- Review proper and common nouns
- Review quotation marks
- Alphabetical order

Materials and Supplies:

- Teacher's Guide & Student Workbook
- White board
- Reader 4: *The Cowboy*

Teaching Tips:

Use the white board to introduce the diphthong **oy** using various beginning consonants or blends. Show how **oy** can be used at the end of a word also.

Activity 1. Study and discuss the pictures in each of the activities. Have the student put a circle around the pictures that have the sound of **oy** as in **boy**.

Pictures: **toy, pray, joy, cowboy**

Activity 2. Finish spelling the words under the pictures by filling in the **oy** sound.

Pictures: cowb**oy**, b**oy**, dec**oy**

Activity 3. Read the words and study the pictures together. Have the student draw a line from the word to the picture it matches.

Pictures: **toy, joy, decoy, Roy**

Activity 4. Read the sentences and the words from the word bank together. Have the student choose the correct word to complete the sentence.

1. The (**cowboy**) lived on a ranch.
2. Which (**toy**) do you like the best.
3. The pants and shirt were for the (**boy**).
4. It is a (**joy**) to hear you sing.

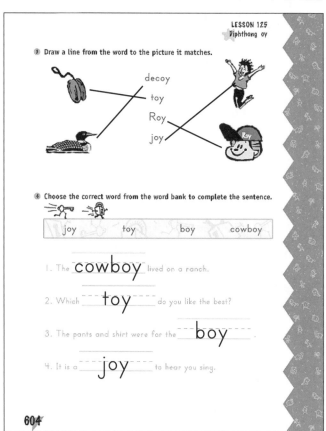

Activity 5. Read the sentences together and discuss proper and common nouns. Have the student draw a LINE under the proper nouns. Put a CIRCLE around the common nouns.

1. Our **dog**, **Spot**, lives in the **barn**.
2. **Dad** took **Paul** and **Roy** to see the **clowns**.
3. The **crew** will row the **boat** across the **lake.**
4. The **hawk** flew to the **nest**.
5. **Gail** and **Jan** will go to the **party**.

Activity 6. Read the sentences together and discuss direct quotations. Have the student put quotation marks around the words that tell what the person is saying.

1. Ben said, ["]What time is it?["]
2. ["]I want to go to the show,["] said Ken.
3. Dad said, ["]We can drive our new truck.["]
4. ["]This is a good horse,["] said the cowboy.

Activity 7. Put the words in alphabetical order.

Words: **boy, enjoy, Roy, toy**

Activity 8. Read each word and then print it under the correct picture.

Pictures: **decoy, joy, Roy**

Activity 9. Read each word with the **oy** sound and then print it.

Words: **joy, enjoy, decoy, boy**

Activity 10. Read one word from each of the rows and have the student put a circle around the correct word in each row.

Words: **joy, jay, coy**
       cowboy, bay, cow
       annoy, Roy, ray
       decoy, destroy, toy

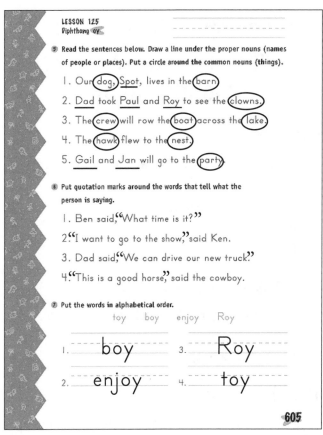

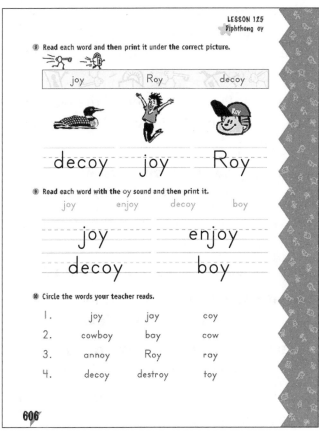

Lesson 126 Review: Digraphs aw, au, ew; Diphthong oy

Overview:

- Review digraphs **aw, au, ew**, and diphthong **oy**
- Sentence completion
- Rhyming
- Printing

Materials and Supplies:

- Teacher's Guide & Student Workbook
- White board
- Reader 4: *Shaw's Camping Trip*

Teaching Tips:

Review and discuss the pictures and digraph sounds in each activity. Encourage the student to work as independently as possible. Make note if there are areas which need to be reinforced.

Activity 1. Put a circle around the pictures that have the sound of **aw** and **au** as in **saw** and **Paul**.

> Pictures: **paw, pail, auto, claw jaw, shawl, heel, haul**

Activity 2. Draw a line from the word to the picture it matches.

> Pictures: **yawn, auto, crawl, paunch**

Activity 3. Put a circle around the pictures that have the **ew** sound as in **few**.

> Pictures: **crew, drew, claw, grew nest, threw, new, chew**

Activity 4. Draw a line from the word to the picture it matches.

> Pictures: **crown, jaw, threw, splash, claw**

Activity 5. Put a circle around the pictures that have the **oy** sound as in **joy**.

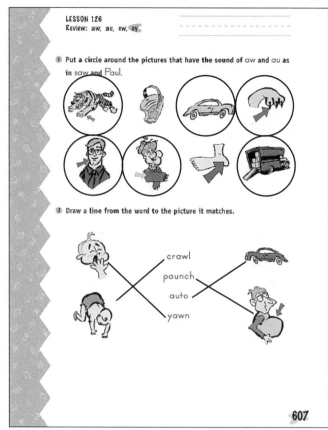

Pictures: **toy, cowboy, box, boy**

Activity 6. Draw a line from the word to the picture it matches.

Pictures: **owl, donkey, Roy, cowboy, money**

Activity 7. Read one word from each of the boxes and have the student put a circle around the correct word in each box.

Words: **jaunt, hawk, flew
chew, cowboy, haul
paw, vault, toy,
new, grew, joy**

Activity 8. Read each word and then write it under the correct picture.

Pictures: **yawn, shawl, crawl**

Activity 9. Read the sentences. Choose the correct word from the word bank to fill in the blanks.

1. Dad will (**haul**) a load of dirt with his truck to the back of the house.
2. I like my (**new**) cowboy shirt and pants.
3. We felt (**joy**) when we sang the songs.
4. The (**claw**) on the hawk was sharp.
5. Did you see the (**crew**) work hard on the roads?
6. A (**fawn**) is a baby deer.
7. The new red (**auto**) can go fast.

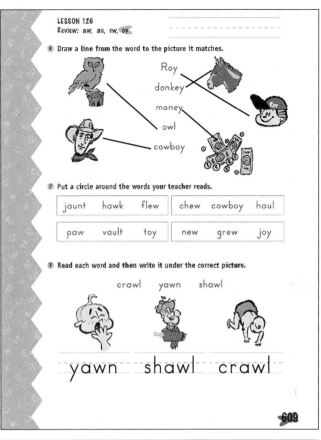

Activity 10. Read each word with the **aw** sound and then write it.

Words: **prawn, law, raw, hawk, fawn, lawn**

Activity 11. Read each word and then write it under the correct picture.

Pictures: **paunch, jaunt, gauze**

Activity 12. Read each word with the **au** sound and then write it.

Words: **Paul, auto, haul, fault, vault, paunch**

Activity 13. Read each word and then write it under the correct picture.

Pictures: **toy, enjoy, destroy**

Activity 14. Read each word with the **oy** sound and then write it.

Words: **cowboy, joy, Roy, decoy**

Activity 15. Print the words from the word bank that rhyme.

chew/**new, few, threw**
dawn/**fawn, drawn, lawn**
jaunt/**gaunt, haunt, taunt**

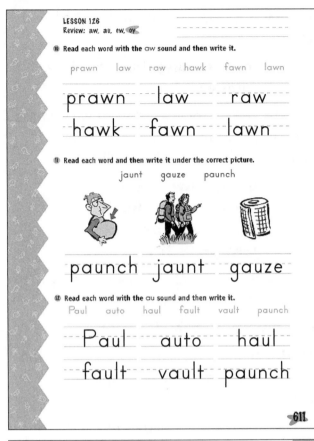

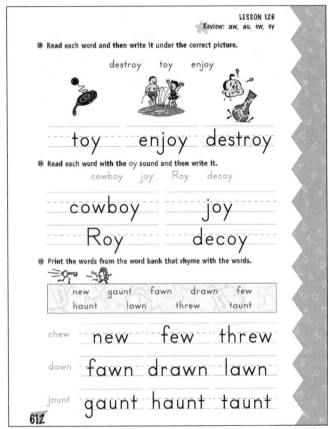

Lesson 127 - Diphthong oi; Sentence Beginning and Ending Punctuation

Overview:

- Diphthong **oi**
- Spelling
- Sentence completion
- Sentence beginning and ending punctuation

Materials and Supplies:

- Teacher's Guide & Student Workbook
- White board
- Reader 4: *Money*

Teaching Tips:

Use the white board to introduce the diphthong **oi** using various beginning consonant or blends.

Review and identify the use of capital letters at the beginning of a sentence and a period or question mark at the end of the sentence.

Activity 1. Introduce the diphthong **oi**. Study and discuss the pictures and words in the activity. Have the student put a circle around the pictures that have the sound of **oi** as in **oil**. Underline the **oi** in each word.

Pictures: **boil, spoil, soil, mouse**
         oink, jaw, point, joint

Activity 2. Read the words and study the pictures together. Discuss the meaning of each word. Have the student draw a line from the word to the picture it matches.

Pictures: **foil, toil, noise, coin, soil**

Activity 3. Practice printing words with **oi** in them. Underline the **oi** in each word.

Words: sp**oi**l, p**oi**nt, b**oi**l, j**oi**n,
       m**oi**st, br**oi**l, t**oi**l, j**oi**nt

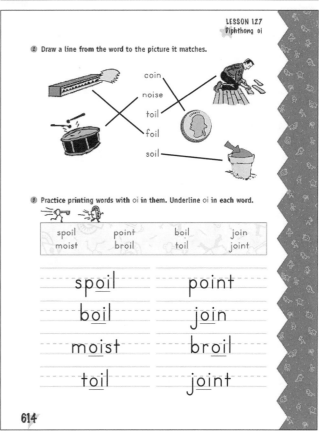

Activity 4. Read the sentences together and discuss the meaning of each. Have the student underline the words that have **oi** in them.

   1. The **soil** is good for the plants to grow.
   2. Jake had a **coin** in his hand.
   3. A car must have **oil** in it to run well.
   4. The **foil** was on top of the food.

Activity 5. Draw a line from the puzzle phrase to the picture it matches.

   Pictures: **point with your foot**
                toil in the oil
                join a pig with an oink

Activity 6. Read the words together. Have the student spell the correct word below each picture. Then print the rest of the words on the lines below.

   Pictures: **poison, coin, joint, voice**

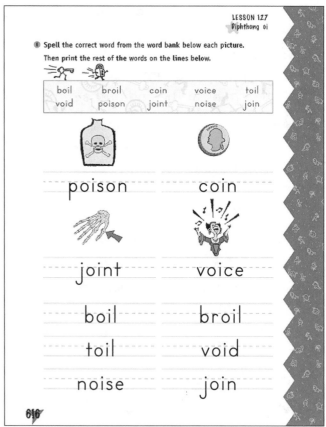

Activity 7. Read the sentences and words together. Have the student choose and print the word that tells about the sentence.

1. Jim is glad he has a good job where he can work. (**toil**)
2. Fern saved her money to put in her bank. (**coin**)
3. We put the meat in the oven to cook. (**broil**)
4. All the boys will meet in the clubhouse. (**join**)
5. Mom cooked the beans in water on top of the stove. (**boil**)
6. The ground was damp. (**moist**)

Activity 8. Discuss using a capital letter to begin each sentence. Review using a period or question mark at the end of each sentence. Read the sentences together. Have the student print the sentences below.

A pig makes the noise we call "oink**."**

Did you join the group**?**

Activity 9. Follow the letters and connect the dots to make a picture. Color the picture.

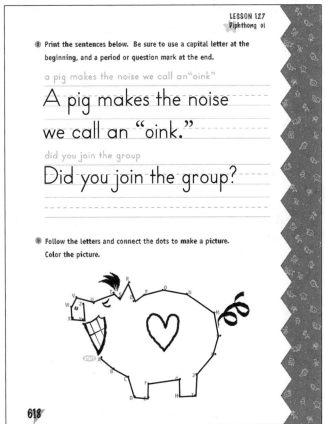

Lesson 128 - Review: Digraphs ay, ey; Diphthongs ou, ow

Overview

- Review digraphs **ay**, **ey** and diphthongs **ow, ou**
- Alphabetical order
- Sentence completion and comprehension
- Rhyming
- Capitalization and punctuation

Materials and Supplies:

- Teacher's Guide & Student Workbook
- White board
- Reader 4: *The Clown*

Teaching Tips:

For all activities, review and discuss the pictures and digraph/diphthong sounds. Encourage the student to work as independently as possible. Make note if there are areas that need to be reinforced.

Activity 1. Put a CIRCLE around the pictures that have the **ow** sound, as in **cow**.

Pictures: **clown, key, owl, howl, crown, down, start, flower**

Activity 2. Put an **X** under the pictures that have the **ow** sound as in **flow** (long **o** sound)

Pictures: **snow, tooth, cloud, show couch, crow, throw, slow**

Activity 3. Put a SQUARE around the pictures that have the **ou** sound as in **house**.

Pictures: **mouse, loud, cloud, monkey scout, grouch, grow, play**

Activity 4. UNDERLINE the pictures that have the **ay** sound as in **stay**.

Pictures: **play, donkey, pray, day, stop, gray, tray, honey**

48

Activity 5. UNDERLINE the pictures that have the **ey** sound as in **valley**.

Pictures: **monkey, toy, key, hockey day, donkey, storm, money**

Activity 6. Put the words in alphabetical order.

Words: **drown, growl, haul, shout**

Activity 7. Choose the correct word to complete the sentence. Print it on the line.

1. The dog will (**stray**) away from home if we are mean to her.
2. The (**monkey**) can swing by its tail.
3. Which (**toy**) do you like the best?
4. We get our milk from the (**cows**).
5. The lady ran from the little gray (**mouse**).

Activity 8. Read one word from each of the rows and have the student put a circle around the correct word in each row.

Words: **couch, town, flower, flour, key, blow, elbow, hound, float, rainbow, pound, stay**

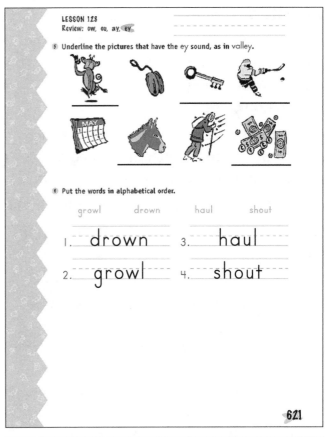

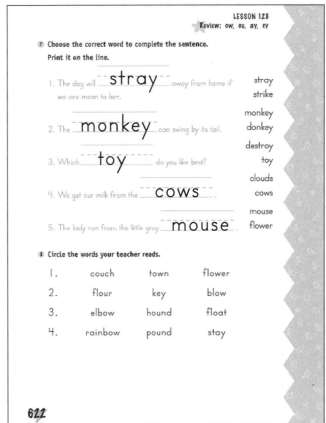

Activity 9. Print the words that rhyme.

owl/**howl, prowl**
cow/**now, plow**
show/**snow, grow**
flour/**hour, sour**

Activity 10. Print the sentence below. Be sure to use a capital letter at the beginning, and a period or question mark at the end.

Will the crowd clap for Dan when he sings**?**

Activity 11. Draw a line from the picture to the sentence it matches.

Pictures: **The crow can fly far away.**
A flower can be yellow, blue, pink, or red.
Where does the owl have its nest?
This pig has a funny snout that sticks out.
All the boys can throw the rocks in the stream.
Did the donkey go back into the barn?

50

Horizons Kindergarten Phonics

Lesson 129 - Review: Digraphs aw, au, ew

Overview:

- Digraphs **aw, au, ew**
- Sentence completion
- Quotation marks
- Spelling

Materials and Supplies:

- Teacher's Guide & Student Workbook
- White board
- Reader 4: *The Fawn*

Teaching Tips:

In all review lessons, go over the pictures and the possible words to accompany the pictures. Encourage the student to work as independently as possible. Take note if there areas in which reinforcement is needed.

Activity 1. Put a circle around the pictures that have the **aw** sound as in **saw**.

Pictures: **shawl, lawn, book, hawk frown, yawn, prawn, claw**

Activity 2. Put a circle around the pictures that have the **au** sound as in **fault**.

Pictures: **haul, broom, Paul, vault auto, couch, gauze, jaunt**

Activity 3. Underline the pictures that have the **ew** sound as in **new**.

Pictures: **chew, jewel, flew, rainbow stool, screw, threw, stew**

Activity 4. Draw a line from the word to the picture it matches.

Pictures: **jewel, fawn, screw, vault**

Activity 5. Choose the correct word to complete the sentence. Print it on the line.

1. The lady (**threw**) the shawl over her arms.
2. Mom has a big (**jewel**) in her ring.
3. Did you help (**throw**) the toys into the chest?
4. When Paul does not get his sleep, we see him (**yawn**).
5. Did the boy (**chew**) his food?
6. The bank has a (**vault**) to keep the money safe.

Activity 6. Print the sentences. Put quotation marks so show the words that are spoken.

1. Paul said, ["]Did you see the hawk?["]
2. ["]No,["] said Ben. ["]I did not see any birds.["]

Activity 7. Draw a line from the puzzle phrase to the picture it matches.

Pictures: **a paw in the vault**
chew the rope
claw the straw
haul a fawn
a screw flew

Activity 8. Spell the correct word below each picture. Then print the rest of the words on the lines below.

Pictures: **stew, claw, paw, haul**

Activity 9. Read one word from each of the rows and have the student put a circle around the correct word in each row.

Words: **jewel, haunt, sauna**
       stew, auto, crawl
       gauze, screw, flaw

Activity 10. Draw a picture. Write a sentence about your picture on the lines below.

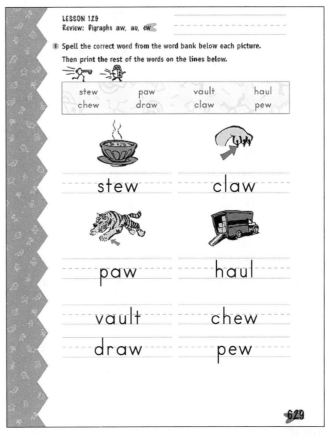

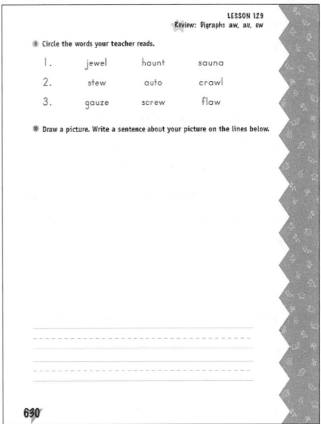

Lesson 130 - Review: Diphthongs ow, ou

Overview:

- Diphthongs **ow, ou**
- Spelling
- Capitalization - Punctuation

Materials and Supplies:

- Teacher's Guide & Student Workbook
- White board
- Reader 4: *The Winner*

Teaching Tips:

In all review lessons, go over the pictures and the possible words to accompany the pictures. Encourage the student to work as independently as possible. Take note if there are areas in which reinforcement is needed.

Activity 1. Put a CIRCLE around the pictures that have the **ow** with a long **o** sound as in **show**.

Pictures: **crow, show, jewel, tow arrow, window, elbow, saw**

Activity 2. UNDERLINE the pictures that have the **ou** sound as in **out**.

Pictures: **hockey, trout, house, mouse sprout, scout, bowl, count**

Activity 3. Draw a line from the word to the picture it matches. Spell the word below each picture.

Pictures: **shadow, pillow, window, arrow**

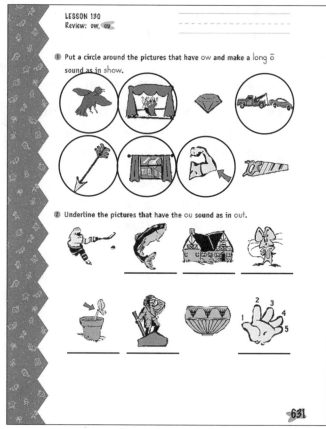

Activity 4. Draw a line from the word to the picture it matches. Spell the word below each picture.

Pictures: **towel, tower, powder, shower**

Activity 5. Put a SQUARE around the pictures that have the **ow** sound as in **how**.

Pictures: **town, powder, key, shower clown, crown, straw, tower**

Activity 6. Read the sentences. Underline the words that have **ou** in them.

1. We live in a new **house**.
2. Dad got a **trout** when he went to the lake to fish.
3. The peach is **round**.
4. The **cloud** in the sky is white.

Activity 7. Read the sentences. Put a CIRCLE around the words that have **ow** and make a long **o** sound.

1. The sun is **low** in the sky.
2. There is a **rainbow** that has **yellow**, blue, and red in it.
3. Jan's left **elbow** hurts.
4. Look out the **window** and you can see the **shadow**.

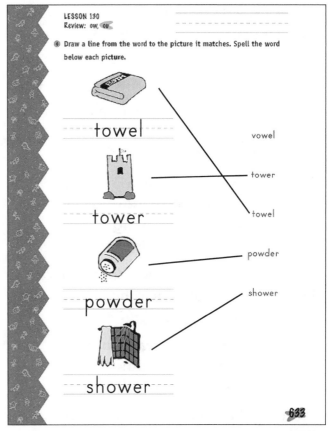

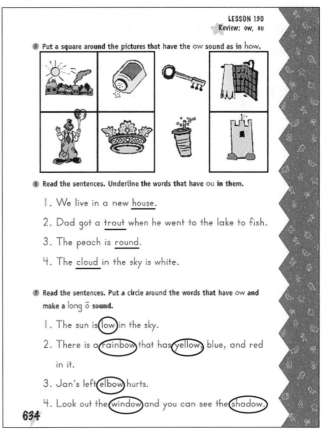

Activity 8. Draw a line from the word to the picture it matches. Spell the word below each picture.

Pictures: **couch, spout, hound, round**

Activity 9. Read one word from each of the rows and have the student put a circle around the correct word in each row.

Words: **pillow, row, blow**
flow, arrow, window
horse, house, hang
yellow, shout, found

Activity 10. Draw a line from the puzzle phrase to the picture it matches.

Pictures: **a bow on a bowl**
a crow on a rainbow
step on a shadow
mow the rocks

Activity 11. Print the sentences. Be sure to use a capital letter at the beginning and a period or question mark at the end of the sentence.

Did you look out the window**?**
Jack is proud to be a **S**cout**.**

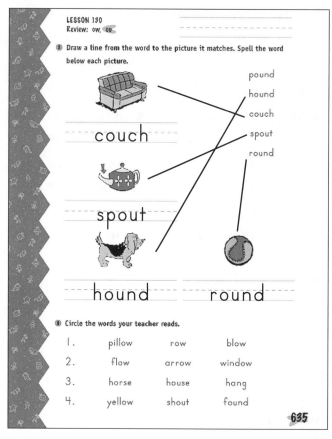

LESSON 130
Review: ow, ou

⑧ Draw a line from the word to the picture it matches. Spell the word below each picture.

pound
hound
couch
spout
round

couch

spout

hound   round

⑨ Circle the words your teacher reads.

1.	pillow	row	blow
2.	flow	arrow	window
3.	horse	house	hang
4.	yellow	shout	found

635

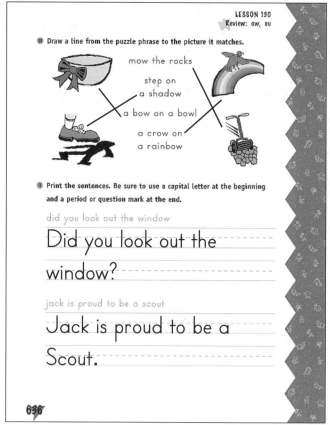

LESSON 130
Review: ow, ou

⑩ Draw a line from the puzzle phrase to the picture it matches.

mow the rocks
step on a shadow
a bow on a bowl
a crow on a rainbow

⑪ Print the sentences. Be sure to use a capital letter at the beginning and a period or question mark at the end.

did you look out the window

Did you look out the window?

jack is proud to be a scout

Jack is proud to be a Scout.

636

Lesson 131 - Review:
Diphthongs oy, oi

Overview:

- Diphthongs **oy**, **oi**
- Spelling
- Rhyming
- Capitalization and punctuation
- Sentence comprehension

Materials and Supplies:

- Teacher's Guide & Student Workbook
- White board
- Reader 4: *The Toy Store*

Teaching Tips:

In all review lessons, go over the pictures and the possible words to accompany the picture. Encourage the student to work as independently as possible. Take note if there are areas in which reinforcement is needed.

Activity 1. Put a circle around the pictures that have the **oy** sound as in **joy**.

> Pictures: **Roy, towel, toy, cowboy
> boil, enjoy, cloud, oink**

Activity 2. Draw a line from the word to the picture it matches. Spell the word below each picture.

> Pictures: **cowboy, annoy, toy, Roy**

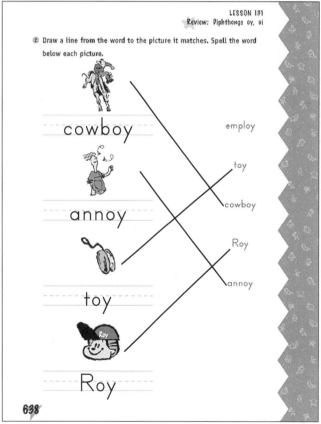

Activity 3. Put a SQUARE around the pictures that have the **oi** sound as in **toil**.

Pictures: **oil, boil, show, voice
cloud, spoil, oink, noise**

Activity 4. Read one word from each of the boxes and have the student put a circle around the correct word in each box.

Words: **toy, boil, joy
spoil, oink, groin
enjoy, annoy, destroy
cowboy, employ, soy**

Activity 5. On the lines below, print the words that rhyme.

oil/**soil, boil, foil**
toy/**destroy, boy, cowboy**

Activity 6. Draw a line from the word to the picture it matches. Spell the word below each picture.

Pictures: **moist, joint, point, noise,
voice, broil**

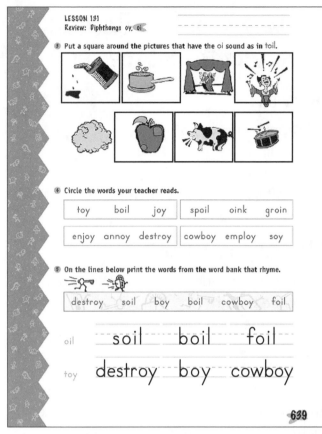

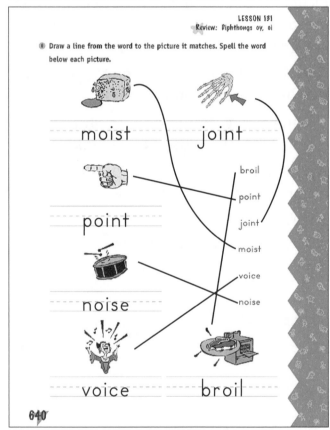

Activity 7. Read the sentences. UNDERLINE the words that have **oy** or **oi** sound in the word.

1. Peg has to **boil** the beets until they are cooked.
2. Dad will **broil** the fish for dinner.
3. The jet crash can **destroy** a house.
4. How many men did the man **employ**?
5. The **cowboy** likes to ride a donkey.
6. The meat will **spoil** if you do not put it away.
7. The man at the shop put **oil** in Dad's auto.

Activity 8. Look at the sentences. On the lines below, print the one sentence that matches the picture.

1. The ground is too moist to plant flowers.
2. Mom will plant beets in the garden.
3. Dad will spray the dirt to make a flower garden.
4. **This plant has sharp points.**

Activity 9. Print the sentences. Be sure to use a capital letter at the beginning and a question mark or period at the end.

When did you put the dinner on to boil**?**
When I get big, I want to be a cowboy**.**

7 Read the sentences. Underline the words that have oy or oi sound in the word.

1. Peg has to boil the beets until they are cooked.
2. Dad will broil the fish for dinner.
3. The jet crash can destroy a house.
4. How many men did the man employ?
5. The cowboy likes to ride a donkey.
6. The meat will spoil if you do not put it away.
7. The man at the shop put oil in Dad's auto.

8 Look at the sentences. On the lines below, print the one sentence that matches the picture.

1. The ground is too moist to plant flowers.
2. Mom will plant beets in the garden.
3. Dad will spray the dirt to make a flower garden.
4. This plant has sharp points.

This plant has sharp points.

641

9 Print the sentences. Be sure to use a capital letter at the beginning and a question mark or period at the end.

when did you put the dinner on to boil

When did you put the dinner on to boil?

when I get big, I want to be a cowboy

When I get big, I want to be a cowboy.

642

Lesson 132 - Letter y as Long i

Overview:

- Introduce Letter **y** as Long **i**
- Spelling
- Sentence completion
- Writing
- Rhyming

Materials and Supplies:

- Teacher's Guide & Student Workbook
- White board
- Reader 4: *A Hot Day in July*

Teaching Tips:

Introduce the letter **y** rule. The letter **y** at the end of a word can change the sound so you hear a long **i**. Use the white board to illustrate as in **my** and **myself**.

Activity 1. Study the pictures together and discuss the meaning of each. Have the student put a circle around the pictures that have the letter **y** that makes the sound of long **i** as in **cry**.

Pictures: **dry, cloud, pry, fry, storm, fly, sky, shy**

Activity 2. Read the words together. Have the student spell the correct word below each picture. Then print the rest of the words on the lines below.

Pictures: **sky, July, shy**

Activity 3. Read one word from each of the boxes and have the student put a circle around the correct word in each box.

Words: **pry, shy, sky**
my, fly, deny
baby, by, dry
sunny, daddy, why

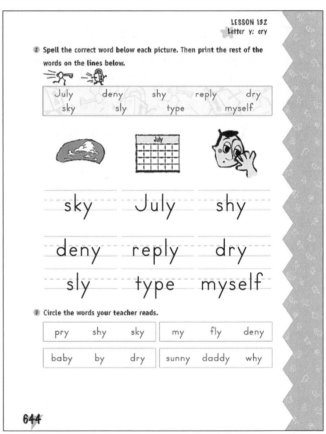

Activity 4. Read the words together. Have the student draw a line from the word to the picture it matches.

Pictures: **cry, fry, dry, fly, type**

Activity 5. Read the sentences together and discuss the meaning. Have the student choose and print the word to make the sentence correct.

1. We were sorry to hear the baby (**cry**).
2. I like to read a book all by (**myself**).
3. The stars are pretty in the (**sky**).
4. Don likes to see the birds (**fly**) to the nests.
5. I will (**try**) to do my best.

Activity 6. Read the sentences and the words in the word bank together. Discuss the meaning of each for comprehension. Have the student print the vocabulary word that tells about the picture.

1. The baby is sad when she goes to bed at night. (**cry**)
2. We did not want to stay wet after we took a bath. (**dry**)
3. Birds do not have to walk or run to get where they want to go. (**fly**)
4. Bill told his mom he did not drop the vase. (**deny**)
5. When someone asks you a question, you must answer. (**reply**)

Activity 7. Write the same sentence by putting your name in place of Dave.

(**Student's name**) will always try to do what is best.

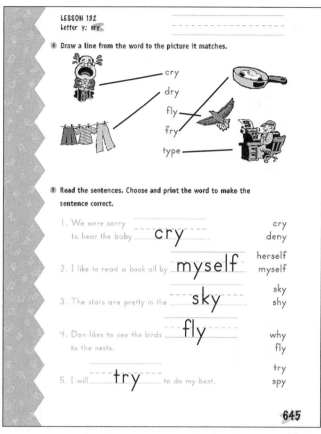

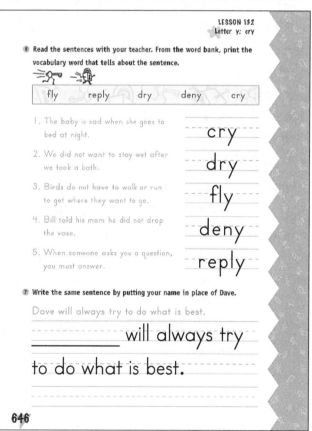

Lesson 133 – Letter y as in baby

Overview

- Introduce Letter **y** as Long **e**
- Spelling
- Rhyming
- Sentence Comprehension
- Writing

Materials and Supplies:

- Teacher's Guide & Student Workbook
- White board
- Reader 4: *The Canary*

Teaching Tips:

Introduce the letter **y** rule. The letter **y** at the end of a word can change the sound and make it say long **e**. Use the white board to illustrate and compare words ending in **y** that have the long **i** sound.

Activity 1. Study the pictures together and discuss the meaning of each. Have the student put a circle around the pictures that have the letter **y** that make the sound of long **e** as in **baby**.

Pictures: **puppy, candy, years, funny paint, marry, study, sorry**

Activity 2. Read the words in the word bank together. Have the student spell the correct word below each picture. Then print the rest of the words on the lines below.

Pictures: **army, skinny, fussy, city, dizzy, empty**

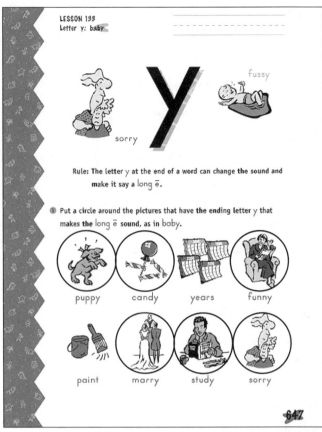

Activity 3. Read the words together and study the pictures. Have the student draw a line from the word to the picture it matches.

Pictures: **cloudy, lucky, rocky, party, rainy, January, sunny**

Activity 4. Print the words that rhyme.

candy/**handy**
sunny/**funny**
rusty/**musty**
marry/**carry**

Activity 5. Read the sentences together. Discuss the words from the word bank that will describe the sentence. Have the student print the vocabulary word that tells about the picture.

1. The baby dog was hungry. (**puppy**)
2. There was not a drop of milk for lunch. (**empty**)
3. Bob got a sweet treat at the store. (**candy**)
4. The merry-go-round made the kids feel funny. (**dizzy**)
5. You can learn a lot when you read books. (**study**)
6. Every day something good happens to me. (**happy**)

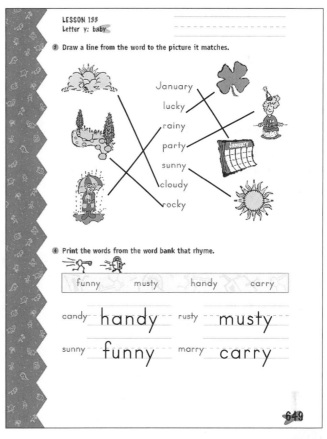

LESSON 133
Letter y: baby

③ Draw a line from the word to the picture it matches.

January
lucky
rainy
party
sunny
cloudy
rocky

④ Print the words from the word bank that rhyme.

| funny | musty | handy | carry |

candy **handy**   rusty **musty**
sunny **funny**   marry **carry**

649

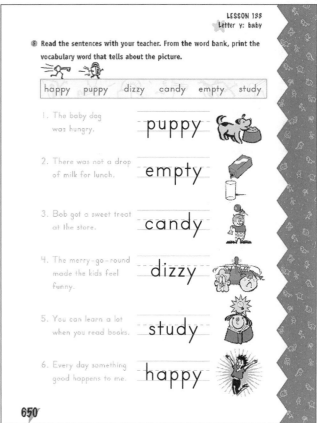

LESSON 133
Letter y: baby

⑤ Read the sentences with your teacher. From the word bank, print the vocabulary word that tells about the picture.

| happy | puppy | dizzy | candy | empty | study |

1. The baby dog was hungry. **puppy**
2. There was not a drop of milk for lunch. **empty**
3. Bob got a sweet treat at the store. **candy**
4. The merry-go-round made the kids feel funny. **dizzy**
5. You can learn a lot when you read books. **study**
6. Every day something good happens to me. **happy**

650

Activity 6. Read the sentences and words together. Have the student choose and print the word to make the sentence correct.

1. The bride and groom will (**marry**) this morning.
2. We could hear the (**puppy**) bark and growl.
3. It makes me (**happy**) when I sing.
4. The (**candy**) was very good to eat.
5. We got wet when we went out on a (**rainy**) day.
6. Don gets (**sleepy**) when he stays up too late.

Activity 7. Read one word from each of the rows and have the student put a circle around the correct word in each row.

Words: **army, baby, happy, fussy, lucky, party sunny, windy, cloudy speedy, tricky, easy**

Activity 8. Write the same sentence by putting your name in place of Becky.

(**Student's name**) said, "I am a lucky person."

⑥ Read the sentences. Choose and print the word to make the sentence correct.

1. The bride and groom will ___marry___ this morning.
   marry
   musty

2. We could hear the ___puppy___ bark and growl.
   rainy
   puppy

3. It makes me ___happy___ when I sing.
   hungry
   happy

4. The ___candy___ was very good to eat.
   candy
   carry

5. We got wet when we went out on a ___rainy___ day.
   rainy
   rocky

6. Don gets ___sleepy___ when he stays up too late.
   shady
   sleepy

651

⑦ Circle the words your teacher reads.

1.	army	baby	happy
2.	fussy	lucky	party
3.	sunny	windy	cloudy
4.	speedy	tricky	easy

⑧ Write the same sentence by putting your name in place of Becky.

Becky said, "I am a lucky person."

652

Lesson 134 - Review: Letter y

Overview:

- Review Letter **y** with both ending sounds
- Auditory discrimination
- Sentence completion
- Capitalization for names
- Creative writing
- Spelling

Materials and Supplies:

- Teacher's Guide & Student Workbook
- White board
- Reader 4: *Benny Bly, the Circus Monkey*

Teaching Tips:

As in all review lessons, go over the pictures and the possible words to accompany the picture. Encourage the student to work as independently as possible. Take note if there are areas in which reinforcement is needed.

Activity 1. Put a CIRCLE around the pictures that have a **y** with the sound of long **i**. Put a SQUARE around the pictures that have a **y** with the sound of long **e**.

Pictures: **candy, fox, sky, baby, happy, tray, puppy, dry**

Activity 2. Read one word from each of the boxes and have the student put a circle around the correct word in each box.

Words: **fussy, lucky, study, puppy, dusty, rainy, cry, try, why funny, marry, many**

Activity 3. Print the words from the word bank in columns.

y with long **e** sound:
puppy, army, baby,study

y with long **i** sound:
deny, July, sky, fry

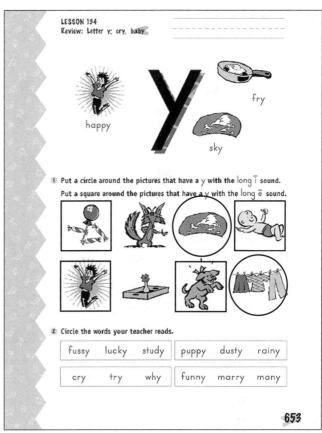

Activity 4. Spell the words under the pictures:

Pictures: **cry, fly, spy**

Activity 5. Choose and print the correct word on the line in each sentence.

1. The (**baby**) will sleep in the crib.
2. I want to see the birds (**fly**) to the trees.
3. My birthday is in (**July**).
4. The milk is all gone so the glass is (**empty**).
5. The girl was so (**skinny**) she had to eat more.
6. All the boys and girls will (**try**) to read the books.
7. The red and yellow roses are (**pretty**).

Activity 6. Print the following sentences using capital letters for the proper nouns.

1. The boy said, "My name is **D**anny."
2. **J**ane has a new puppy.
3. Lots of boys and girls live in the state of **M**aine.

Activity 7. Help the student create a sentence using his own name.

LESSON 134
Review: Letter y; ory, baby

5 Choose and print the correct word on the line in each sentence.

1. The ___baby___ will sleep in the crib. baby type

2. I want to see the birds ___fly___ to the trees. easy fly

3. My birthday is in ___July___ defy July

4. The milk is all gone so the glass is ___empty___ empty enemy

5. The girl was so ___skinny___ she had to eat more. skinny why

6. All the boys and girls will ___try___ to read the books. try very

7. The red and yellow roses are very ___pretty___ party pretty

655

LESSON 134
Review: Letter y; ory, baby

6 Print the following sentences using capital letters for the proper nouns.

The boy said, "My name is danny."

The boy said, "My name is Danny."

jane has a new puppy.

Jane has a new puppy.

Lots of boys and girls live in the state of maine.

Lots of boys and girls live in the state of Maine.

7 Have your teacher help you write a sentence using your own name.

656

Lesson 135 - Vowel Digraph oo as in look

Overview:

- Introduce the vowel digraph with both sounds as in **book** and **tooth**
- Writing
- Rhyming
- Sentence completion
- Vocabulary development

Materials and Supplies:

- Teacher's Guide & Student Workbook
- White board
- Reader 4: *Wooley*

Teaching Tips:

Introduce the vowel digraph **oo** with both sounds: as in **book** and as in **tooth**.

Use the white board to illustrate the various beginnings and endings. Allow the student to create his own make-up word and practice both sounds within. Show him the option of "If one doesn't work, try the other one." In this lesson, concentration will be centered on the **oo** sound as in **book**.

Activity 1. Read the words and study the pictures together. Have the student print the word on the line below each picture.

Pictures: **hook, hood, foot, stood, brook, book**

Activity 2. Read the sentences together. Have the student underline the words that have the short **oo** sound as in **book**.

1. I **took** so long to get ready that I was late.
2. The **nook** in the park had benches made of **wood**.
3. Did you take a **look** in that big red **book**?
4. There is a **crook** in the branch of the tree.
5. Mom can **cook** the meat just the say we like it.
6. We were so cold we **shook** all over.
7. Dave had a **hood** on his coat.
8. My **foot** has five toes.
9. The farmers shear the **wool** from the sheep every year.
10. There were many fish swimming in the **brook**.
11. The baby **stood** too close to the pond.

Activity 3. Read one word from each of the boxes and have the student put a circle around the correct word in each box.

Words: **good, soot, crook book, took, shook cook, wool, look, stood, hood, wood**

Activity 4. Read each word and then write it under the correct picture.

Pictures: **foot, cook book, stood**

Activity 5. Print the words that rhyme.

good/**wood, stood, hood**
cook/**book, took, look**

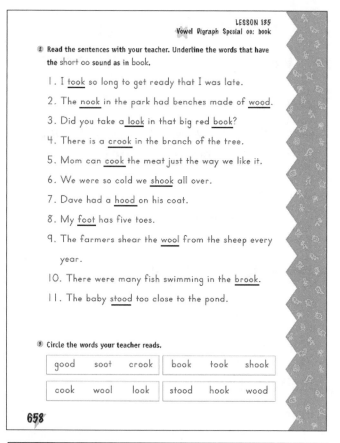

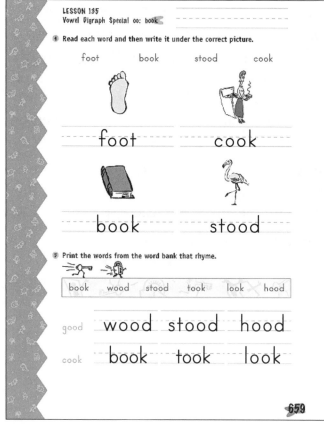

Activity 6. Read the sentences together and discuss the meaning of each. Have the student print the vocabulary word that tells about the sentence.

1. It is a good idea to study the things you read in school. (**book**)
2. We went to a special place in the park to watch the birds. (**nook**)
3. Hang your coat up every time you take it off. (**hook**)
4. You have to get your meals ready to eat. (**cook**)
5. Dan can fish in many other places than just a lake or pond. (**brook**)
6. He did not want to sit down; he wanted to stand up. (**stood**)

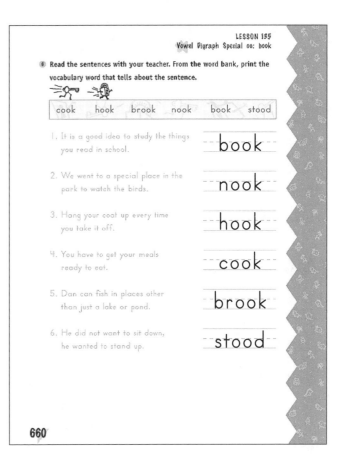

Lesson 136 - Vowel Digraph oo as in tooth

Overview:

- Introduce the digraph **oo** as in **tooth**
- Sentence comprehension
- Writing
- Rhyming
- Vocabulary development

Materials and Supplies:

- Teacher's Guide & Student Workbook
- White board
- Reader 4: *The Black Widow Spider*

Teaching Tips:

Review the rule for vowel digraph **oo** with both sounds: as in **book**; and as in **tooth**. Use the white board to illustrate the various beginnings and endings. Allow the student to create his own make-up word and practice both sounds within. Show him the option of if one doesn't work, try the other one. In this lesson concentration will be centered on the **oo** sound as in **tooth**.

Activity 1. Read the words and pictures together and discuss the meanings of each. Have the student read each word under the picture and then write it on the lines below.

Pictures: **zoo, food, drool
spool, tool, school**

Activity 2. Read the sentences together. Have the student underline the words that have the long **oo** sound as in tooth.

1. The baby got his first **tooth** when he was six months old.
2. We saw all the animals at the **zoo**.
3. It was such a **cool** day, we had to wear our coats.
4. Did you hear the cow **moo**?
5. The **hoof** on the horse was broken.
6. Dad had to fix the **roof** because there was a leak in it.
7. Cats like to play with a **spool** on a string.
8. The boys and girls had played so hard they had to **snooze**.
9. The rocks and stones were worn **smooth**.
10. It is fun to swim in a **pool**.

Activity 3. Read one word from each of the rows and have the student put a circle around the correct word in each row.

Words: **root, boost, moose**
　　　shoot, boot, tooth,
　　　zoo, school, stool
　　　spoon, spool, bloom

Activity 4. Read each word and then write it under the correct picture.

Pictures: **root, moose, roof, tooth**

Activity 5. Print the sentence on the lines below.

Sentence: **I stay in a very good mood.**

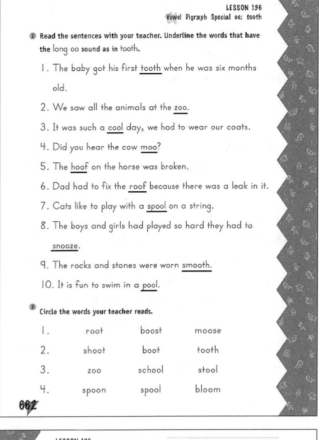

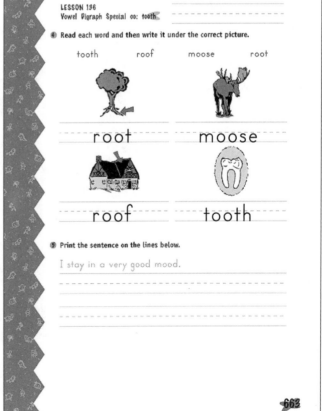

Activity 6. Print the words that rhyme

loose/**moose, noose**
root/**toot, boot**
coop/**stoop, droop**

Activity 7. Read the sentences and words together. Discuss the meaning for vocabulary development and concentration. Have the student choose a word from the word bank that tells about the sentence.

1. Wild animals live in a nice place where people can see them. (**zoo**)
2. Hens and roosters need a place to live and eat their food. (**coop**)
3. There is a wild animal with huge horns that can run very fast. (**moose**)
4. We need to eat the right things to stay healthy. (**food**)

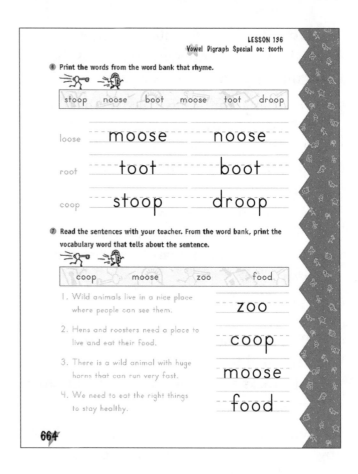

Lesson 137 - Review All Digraphs/Diphthongs

Overview

- Review all digraphs and diphthongs
- Spelling
- Common nouns
- Sentence comprehension

Materials and Supplies:

- Teacher's Guide & Student Workbook
- White board
- Reader 4: *Pointer, the Watchdog*

Teaching Tips:

As in all review lessons, go over the pictures and the possible words to accompany the picture. Review all the digraphs. Review common nouns. Encourage the student to work as independently as possible. Take note if there are areas in which reinforcement is needed.

Activity 1. Spell the words under the pictures by choosing the correct digraph or diphthong sound.

> Pictures: tr**ay**, pr**ay**, spr**ay**
> mon**ey**, t**oy**, b**oy**
> c**ow**, cl**ow**n, gr**ay**
> t**oo**th, b**oo**t, cl**ay**

Activity 2. Spell the words under the pictures by choosing the correct digraph or diphthong sound.

> Pictures: j**aw**, cl**aw**, b**oi**l
> b**oo**k, sh**oo**k, f**oi**l
> v**au**lt, h**au**l, cowb**oy**
> k**ey**, j**oy**, donk**ey**

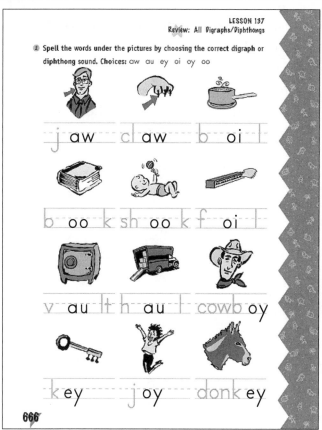

Activity 3. Spell the words under the pictures by choosing the correct digraph sound.

Pictures: gr**ow**, m**ow**, h**oo**k
        sm**oo**th, sl**ow**, cr**ew**

Activity 4. Circle the common nouns in each sentence that name a thing.

1. The **claw** of the **bird** is yellow.
2. Where did the **boy** go?
3. Jane had a blue **shawl**.
4. The **vault** is full of **money**.
5. Dad put a **screw** in the **desk**.

Activity 5. Read the sentences below. Draw a line from the picture that matches the sentence.

1. The monkey gave the tray to the clown.
2. Peg wants gray clay to make the bowl for the flowers.
3. The donkey had a broken tooth in his jaw.
4. Drew took the book to school to show the other boys.
5. The cowboy took the rope out of the coil to catch the donkey.
6. The crew that will row the boat is in town.

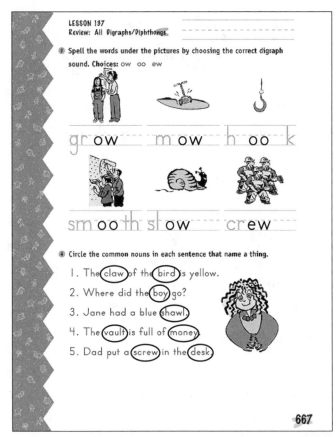

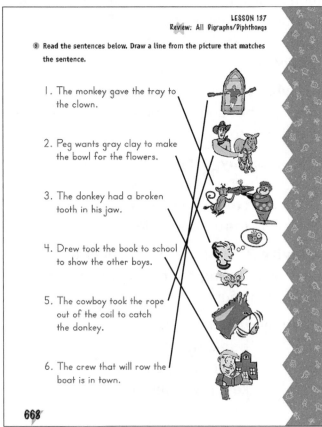

Lesson 138 - Review: Letter y; Digraphs ay, ey; Diphthongs oy, oi

Overview

- Review letter **y** with both sounds of long **i** and **e**; digraphs **ay, ey**; diphthongs **oy, oi**
- Spelling/Rhyming
- Sentence completion
- Printing

Materials and Supplies:

- Teacher's Guide & Student Workbook
- White board
- Reader 4: *The Muddy Pond*

Teaching Tips:

As in all review lessons, go over the pictures and the possible words to accompany the picture. Review the digraphs and diphthongs. Encourage the student to work as independently as possible.

Activity 1. Spell the words under the pictures by choosing the correct digraph or diphthong sound.

Pictures: fl**y**, j**oy**, t**oy**
    pr**ay**, tr**ay**, sk**y**

Activity 2. Print the sentence using your name.

(**Student's name**) is happy when reading a schoolbook.

Activity 3. Spell the words under the pictures by choosing the correct digraph or diphthong sound.

Pictures: c**oi**l, monk**ey**, pl**ay**
    k**ey**, f**oi**l, gr**ay**

Activity 4. Read one word from each of the rows and have the student put a circle around the correct word in each row.

Words: **funny, baby, bunny,**

Horizons Kindergarten Phonics

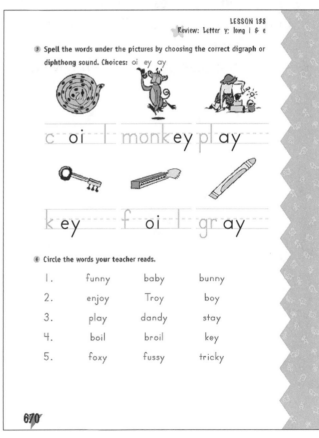

enjoy, Troy, boy,
play, dandy, stay,
boil, broil, key
foxy, fussy, tricky

Activity 5. Spell the words under the pictures by choosing the correct diphthong sound.

Pictures: pupp**y**, bab**y**, cowb**oy**
destr**oy**, d**ay**, x-r**ay**

Activity 6. Print the words that rhyme.

sandy/**handy**
key/**monkey**
joy/**coy**
toil/**coil**
stay/**tray**
lady/**shady**

Activity 7. Choose and print the correct word to complete the sentence.

1. Dad will (**pay**) money so I can ride the horses.
2. Bobby keeps his (**toy**) in the trunk.
3. Donny will (**try**) to lift the window.
4. The (**monkey**) lives in the zoo.
5. I hope you did not (**soil**) your dress when you fell.
6. We ate the (**candy**) that Mom gave us.

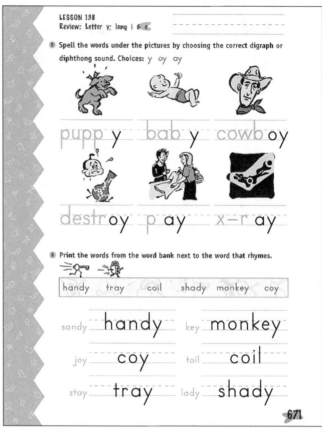

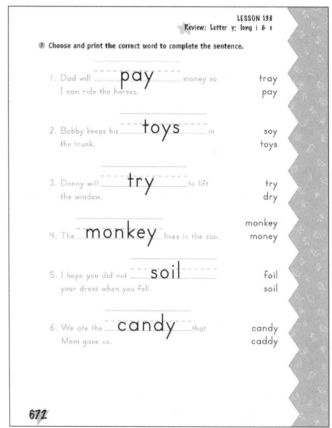

Horizons Kindergarten Phonics

Lesson 139 - Silent W

Overview

- Introduce silent **w**
- Spelling
- Sentence comprehension
- Creative sentence writing

Materials and Supplies:

- Teacher's Guide & Student Workbook
- White Board
- Reader 4: *The Wristwatch*

Teaching Tips:

Use the white board to introduce the Silent **W** Rule. Show the student how to cross out the **w** and begin the word with the sound of **r**.

Activity 1. Introduce the Silent **W** Rule: When **w** is followed by **r**, the **w** is silent. Read the words and study the pictures together. Have the student read each word and then write it on the line below. Cross out the silent **w**.

> Pictures: **wrench, wrist, wring, wrinkle, writer, wrestler**

Activity 2. Read the words together and discuss the meaning of each. Have the student spell the correct word beside each picture. Then print the rest of the words on the lines below.

> Pictures: **wrong, wren, wrapper**

Activity. 3. Look at the words below. When is the **w** silent? Draw a line under the words that have a silent **w**.

> Words: **wrist, write**, wood, swift, **wrench, wren**

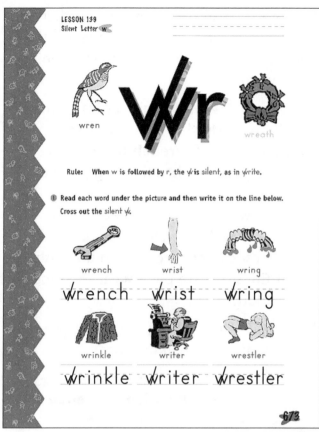

Activity 4. Read the sentences together and discuss the meaning of each. Underline the words that have a silent **w** at the beginning of the word.

1. Dave will **wrap** the gift for his mom.
2. The **wrestler** has strong **wrists**.
3. Dad needed a **wrench** to fix his car.
4. The little **wren** had three eggs in her nest.
5. We saw two cars in a **wreck**.
6. I like to **write** a note to my pals.
7. The candy **wrapper** was in the trash.
8. At Christmas we put a **wreath** in the window.

Activity 5. Draw a line from the puzzle phrase to the picture it matches.

Pictures: **two wrists on an arm**
a wrestler with a wrench
write with a wrench
a wreath on a wren

Activity 6. Look at the picture of a boy writing a letter. Tell your teacher two things about the picture. Then write a sentence of your own on the lines.

Activity 7. Read one word from each of the boxes and have the student put a circle around the correct word in each box.

Words: **wrestle, rest, fist**
wrap, wrapper, trap
wrong, wrist, first
wren, hen, went
wreck, track, prank
wrist, test, tent

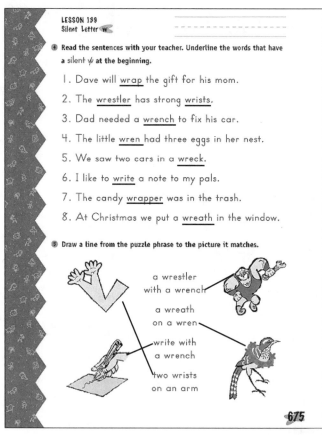

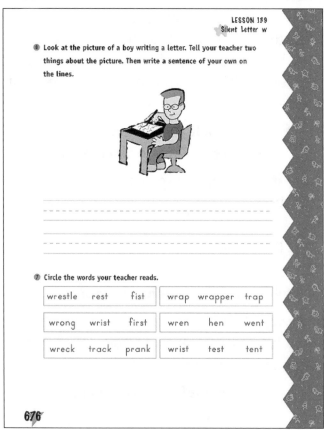

Lesson 140 - Silent K

Overview

- Introduce Silent **K**
- Spelling
- Sentence comprehension
- Creative sentence writing

Materials and Supplies:

- Teacher's Guide & Student Workbook
- White Board
- Reader 4: *A Knock at the Door*

Teaching Tips:

Use the white board to introduce the Silent **K** Rule. Show the student how to cross out the **k** and begin the word with the sound of **n**.

Activity 1. Introduce the Silent **K** Rule: When **k** is followed by **n**, the **k** is silent. Read the words and study the pictures together. Have the student read each word and then write it on the lines below. Cross out the silent **k**.

> Pictures: **knock, knit, knuckle knot, knee, knob**

Activity 2. Read the words together and discuss the meaning of each. Have the student spell the correct word below each picture. Then print the rest of the words on the lines below.

> Pictures: **kneel, knead, knot**

Activity 3. Draw a line from the puzzle phrase to the picture it matches.

> Phrases: **a knob that knocks
> knead with knuckles
> knit a knapsack
> a knee in a knot**

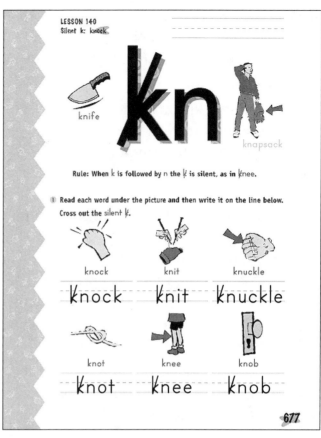

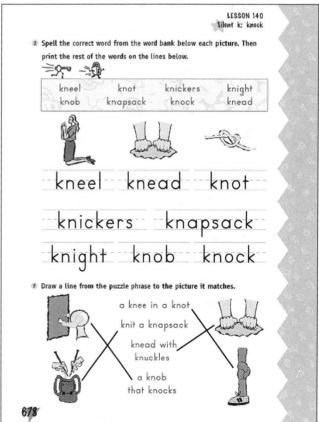

Activity 4. Read the sentences with together and discuss the meaning of each. Have the student underline the words that have a silent **k** at the beginning.

1. Can you tie **knots** in the string?
2. I **knew** that secret a long time ago.
3. Did you hear the **knock** at the door?
4. The **knob** on the front door will not work.
5. What will you put in your **knapsack** for camping?
6. My mom can **knit** a coat.
7. We cut the cake with a sharp **knife**.
8. People used to wear **knickers** for pants.
9. Jill got on her **knees** to say a prayer.
10. I **know** I like to read and write.

Activity 5. Read one word from each of the rows and have the student put a circle around the correct word in each row.

Words: **knob, knock, lock**
      knit, kit, pink
      knuckle, buckle, kick
      knee, cheek, stream
      knot, knew, knife
      know, show, now

Activity 6. Look at the words below. When is the **k** silent? Draw a line under the words that have a silent **k**.

Words: **knife, knit,** kitten, kite, **knock**

Activity 7. Look at the picture of a boy and girl on their knees in prayer. Tell your teacher two things about the picture. Then write a sentence of your own on the lines.

LESSON 140
Silent k: knock

④ Read the sentences with your teacher. Underline the words that have a silent k̶ at the beginning.

1. Can you tie <u>knots</u> in the string?
2. I <u>knew</u> that secret a long time ago.
3. Did you hear the <u>knock</u> at the door?
4. The <u>knob</u> on the front door will not work.
5. What will you put in your <u>knapsack</u> for camping?
6. My mom can <u>knit</u> a coat.
7. We cut the cake with a sharp <u>knife</u>.
8. People used to wear <u>knickers</u> for pants.
9. Jill got on her <u>knees</u> to say a prayer.
10. I <u>know</u> I like to read and write.

⑤ Circle the words your teacher reads.

1.	knob	knock	lock
2.	knit	kit	pink
3.	knuckle	buckle	kick
4.	knee	cheek	stream
5.	knot	knew	knife
6.	know	show	now

679

LESSON 140
Silent k: knock

⑥ Look at the words below. When is the k silent? Draw a line under the words that have a silent k̶.

<u>knife</u>   <u>knit</u>   kitten   kite   <u>knock</u>

⑦ Look at the picture of a boy and girl on their knees in prayer. Tell your teacher two things about the picture. Then write a sentence of your own on the lines.

680

Lesson 141 - Silent B

Overview

- Introduce Silent **B**
- Spelling
- Sentence comprehension
- Sentence creation

Materials and Supplies:

- Teacher's Guide & Student Workbook
- White board
- Reader 4: *Crumbs for the Birds*

Teaching Tips:

When introducing the Silent **B**, use the white board to illustrate. Call attention to the sound of **m** when completing the word.

Activity 1. Introduce the Silent **B** Rule: When **mb** is at the end of a word, the **b** is silent, as in **comb**. Read and discuss the meaning of each word. Have the student print it on the lines below. Cross out the silent **b**.

Pictures: **comb, bomb, thumb**
lamb, limb, climb

Activity 2. Read the words together and discuss each meaning. Have the student spell the correct word below each picture. Then print the rest of the words on the lines below.

Pictures: **climb, bomb, limb**

Activity 3. Read the puzzle phrases together. Have the student draw a line from the phrase to the picture it matches.

Phrases: **a limb on a crumb**
a thumb crushing a crumb
a lamb with a comb
a dumb thumb

Activity 4. Read one word from each of the rows and have the student put a circle around the correct word in each row.

Words: **thumb, comb, wrist**
numb, wrinkle, knuckle
lamb, numb, knit
bomb, limb, write
tomb, time, wren

Activity 5. Read the sentences together. Have the student underline the words that have a silent **b** at the end.

1. The birds will eat all the **crumbs**.
2. My **thumb** is broken.
3. The man will **plumb** the kitchen sink.
4. The **bomb** will go off at seven.
5. She felt **numb** when she saw the **bomb**.
6. Can the baby **climb** the tree?
7. The baby **lamb** will be big next spring.
8. It is **dumb** to think you are **dumb**. You are smart.
9. Jan can fix her hair with her new **comb**.

Activity 6. Look at the words below. When is the **b** silent? Draw a line under the words that have a silent **b**.

Words: **thumb**, stub, bulb, **plumb**, **comb**

Activity 7. Look at the picture of twin lambs playing in a park. The mother wants the twins to come home to the barn. Tell your teacher something about the picture. Then write a sentence of your own on the lines below.

LESSON 141
Silent b: thumb

④ Circle the words your teacher reads.

1.	thumb	comb	wrist
2.	numb	wrinkle	knuckle
3.	lamb	numb	knit
4.	bomb	limb	write
5.	tomb	time	wren

⑤ Read the sentences with your teacher. Underline the words that have a silent b at the end.

1. The birds will eat all the crumbs.
2. My thumb is broken.
3. The man will plumb the kitchen sink.
4. The bomb will go off at seven.
5. She felt numb when she saw the bomb.
6. Can the baby climb the tree?
7. The baby lamb will be big next spring.
8. It is dumb to think you are dumb. You are smart.
9. Jan can fix her hair with her new comb.

683

LESSON 141
Silent b: thumb

⑥ Look at the words below. When is the b silent? Draw a line under the words that have a silent b.

thumb   stub   bulb   plumb   comb

⑦ Look at the picture of twin lambs playing in a park. The mother wants the twins to come home to the barn. Tell your teacher something about the picture. Then write a sentence of your own on the lines below.

684

Horizons Kindergarten Phonics

Lesson 142 - Review: Silent Letters b, k, w; Letter Writing

Overview:

- Review Silent **B** and **K**
- Sentence Comprehension
- Letter Writing

Materials and Supplies:

- Teacher's Guide & Student Workbook
- White board
- Reader 4: *A Knitted Coat*

Teaching Tips:

Review the Silent **B** and **K** before beginning the lesson. Use the white board to illustrate letter writing. Discuss parts of a letter.

Activity 1. Review Silent **B** and **K**. Have the student put a CIRCLE around the words that have a silent **b** Put a SQUARE around the words that have a silent **k**. UNDERLINE the words that have a silent **w**.

silent **b**: **bomb, comb, climb, crumb**
silent **k**: **knit, knife, knob, knot**
silent **w**: **write, wrong, wrist, wring,
     wrestler, wrap**

Activity 2. Draw a line from the word to the picture it matches. Then spell the word below the picture.

Pictures: **knob, write, wrap, knit, comb**

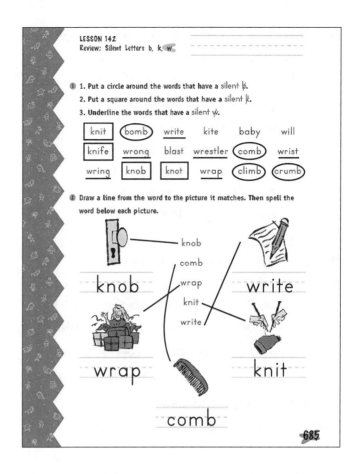

Activity 3. Read one word from each of the rows and have the student put a circle around the correct word in each row.

Words: **kitten, blast, bomb**
want, wrap, ship
write, cowboy, broil
king, kite, knife
comb, joy, came
knot, pry, play

Activity 4. From the word bank, circle all the words that have a silent letter in them. Print the words that you have circled on the lines below. Put a line through the silent letters in each of the words you have printed.

Silent-letter words: **climb, wrist, know**
kneel, comb, wrote

Activity 5. Read the sentences together. Have the student draw a line to the picture that matches the sentence.

1. We will write a note to say thank you for the party.
2. Mom had to use a knife to fix the peaches for the pie.
3. The noise was so loud it sounded like a bomb.
4. The wrestler came to town to show his skills.
5. I will wrap the gift for my mom.
6. Men used to wear knickers instead of pants.
7. Did you comb your hair a new way?

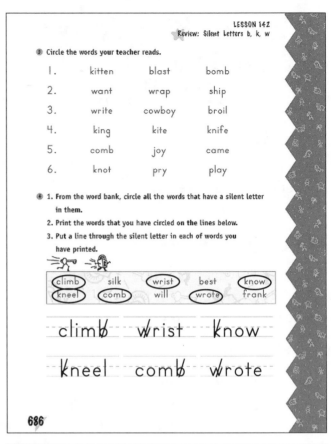

Activity 6. Discuss the picture and read the letter together. Talk about invitations and the need to respond to an invitation. Have the student make note of the indentation, salutation, body, and closing placement in the letter.

Activity 7. Discuss letter writing. Have the student create a letter in response to a party invitation. Print it on the lines below.

⑥ Look at the picture. It tells about Nan getting a letter from Jane. In the letter Jane asked Nan to come to her house for her sixth birthday party. Nan is happy. She wants to go. Read the note with your teacher.

Dear Nan,

    I will be six years old on Monday, June 14th. I would like to have you come to my party at 2:00 P.M. The party will be held at my house. Please let me know if you would like to come.

               Your friend,
               Jane

688

⑦ Talk with your teacher about how you can send a note to Jane telling her that you would like to go to the party. Print it on the lines below.

Dear _____,

_____

_____

_____

_____

_____

         Your friend,

        _____

689

Activity 8.

Draw a picture of Jane's birthday party.

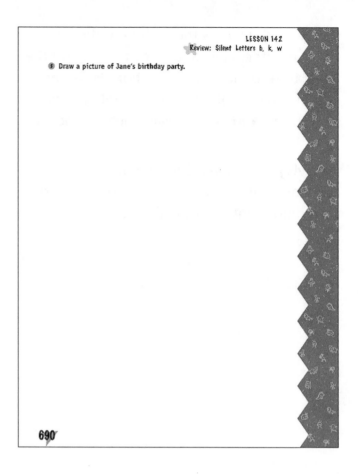

⑧ Draw a picture of Jane's birthday party.

690

Horizons Kindergarten Phonics

Lesson 143 - Silent G; Writing Question Sentences

Overview

- Introduce Silent **G**
- Spelling
- Sentence comprehension
- Writing question sentences

Materials and Supplies:

- Teacher's Guide & Student Workbook
- White board
- Reader 4: *Watch the Signs and Newspaper Headlines*

Teaching Tips:

Use the white board to introduce the Silent **g** Rule. Explain that when the beginning letters are **gn**, the **g** is silent as in **gnat**. Review how this is the same principle as in **kn**, and **wr**.

Discuss the paragraph about swimming. Develop question sentences related to safety.

Activity 1. Introduce the Silent **G** Rule: When the letter **g** is followed by **n** in a word, the **g** is silent as in **gnat**. Read the words together and discuss the meaning of each. Have the student notice that **gn** does not have to be at the beginning of the word, as in sign. Print the word on the lines below the picture. Cross out the silent **g**.

Pictures: **gnash, gnu, gnat gnaw, sign, gnarl**

Activity 2. Read the words together. Have the student spell the correct word below each picture and then print the rest of the words on the lines below.

Pictures: **gnarl, gnash, gnaw**

Activity 3. Read one word from each of the rows and have the student put a circle around the correct word in each row.

Horizons Kindergarten Phonics

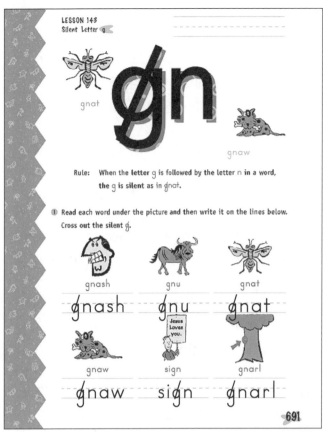

Words: **sign, sing, ring
write, comb, gnash
gnat, get, knee
gnaw, keep, numb**

Activity 4. Read the sentences together. Have the student underline the words that have **gn** in them. Draw a line from the sentence to the picture it matches.

1. A **gnat** is an insect that can bite and sting.
2. The shark looked like he would **gnash** his teeth.
3. Spot, the dog, will **gnaw** on any bone he finds.
4. A **gnu** has horns and a head like an ox.
5. A **gnarl** is a hard knot on the trunk of a tree.
6. Dad must stop his car when he sees a stop **sign**.

Activity 5. Read the words together in the word bank. Have the student (1) Circle all the words that have a silent letter in them. (2) Print the words that have been circled on the lines below. (3) Put a line through the silent letter in each of the words printed.

Silent-letter words:

comb, wring, knit, knee, lamb, wrestle, sign, gnat, climb, gnarl, gnu, plumb

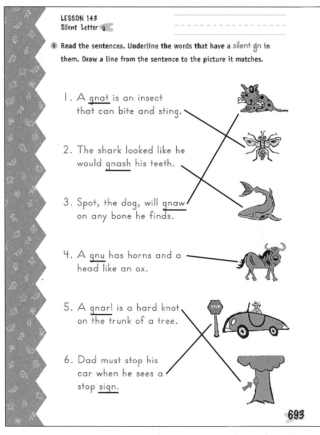

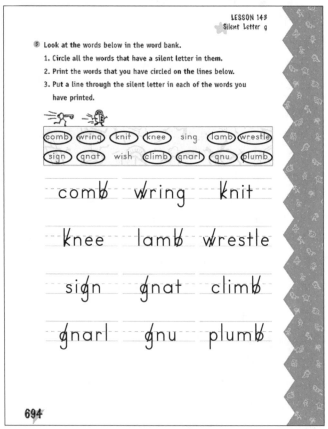

Horizons Kindergarten Phonics

Activity 6. Discuss the picture of Mike diving from the side of the swimming pool. Read the questions below. Talk about other safety questions.

1. Does Mike have someone with him?
2. Is the water too deep?
3. Does Mike know how to swim?
4. Did he read all of the signs?

Activity 7. Discuss other questions that could be asked. Help the student print one on the lines below. Be sure to put a capital letter on the first word and a question mark at the end of the sentence.

Activity 8.

Draw a picture.

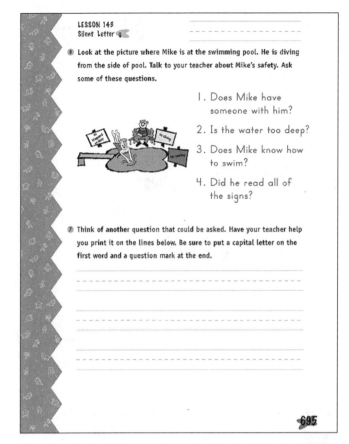

Lesson 144 - Silent gh

Overview

- Introducing Silent **gh**
- Spelling
- Sentence comprehension

Materials and Supplies:

- Teacher's Guide & Student Workbook
- White board
- Reader 4: *The Big Cats*

Teaching Tips:

Use the white board to introduce the Silent **gh** Rule. Explain that when the word ends the letters **igh** or **ight**, the **i** is long, and the **gh** is silent.

Activity 1. Introduce the Silent **gh** Rule. Read the words together and discuss the meaning of each. Have the student notice the placement of **igh** and **ight** coming at the end of the word. (1) Put a circle around the pictures that have a silent **gh**. (2) Cross out the silent letters **gh** in each word.

Pictures: **night, thigh, flight, height, high, right, sight, light**

Activity 2. Finish spelling the word under each picture by filling in the beginning and ending letters.

Pictures: **n**igh**t**, **h**ig**h**, **s**igh**t**

Activity 3. Finish spelling the word under each picture by filling in the middle letters in each word.

Pictures: **r**igh**t**, **l**igh**t**, **fl**igh**t**

Activity 4. Draw a line from the phrase to the picture it matches.

Pictures: **a right turn**
a dim light
a stop sign
a tight dress

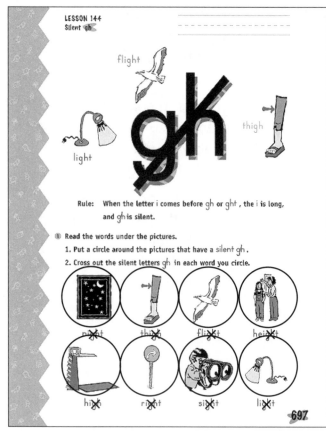

Activity 5. Read the sentences together and discuss the meaning of each. (1) Have the student draw a line under the sentence that matches the picture. (2) Print the correct sentence on the lines below.

It is too late at night to take a ride.
It is too late at right to take a ride.

Please stop at the gnat sign.
Please stop at the stop sign.

The wrestlers had a fight in the ring.
The wrestlers had a light in the wrong.

Activity 6. Read one word from each of the rows and have the student put a circle around the correct word in each row.

Words: **flight, flat, fight**
       sign, sight, stop
       right, wrong, gnat
       light, lamp, look

Activity 7. Discuss the picture. Help the student identify two things that use the **ight** words you have had in this lesson. Put a circle around those two things and print the words on the lines below.

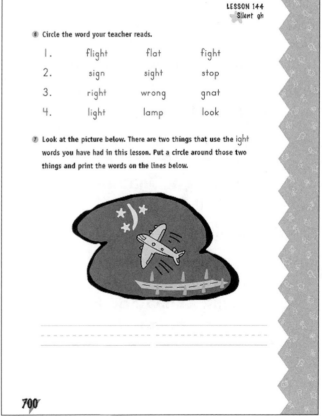

Lesson 145 - Review Silent w, k, b, gn, gh

Overview

- Review of Silent **w**, **k**, **b**, **gn**, and **gh**
- Writing creative sentences

Materials and Supplies:

- Teacher's Guide & Student Workbook
- White board
- Reader 4: *The Wrong Count*

Teaching Tips:

Review the entire lesson and then allow the student to work as independently as possible. Make note of any areas in which reinforcement is needed.

Activity 1. Read the words under the pictures. Underline the silent letter(s) in each word.

Pictures: **w**rit**e**, **k**nif**e**, com**b**, si**g**n,
   wrist, **g**nat, **k**ne**e**, crum**b**

Activity 2. Read the words. Underline the silent letter(s) in each word.

Words: **k**ne**e**, **k**nuckl**e**, **k**nit
   wrist, **w**rinkl**e**, **w**rong
   sli**gh**t, ni**gh**t, si**gh**t
   com**b**, thum**b**, num**b**

Activity 3. Print the words in rows:

Silent **g** words: **gnu, gnash**
Silent **gh** words: **flight, light**
Silent **k** words: **knapsack, knit**
Silent **b** words: **bomb, climb**
Silent **w** words: **wrench, wring**

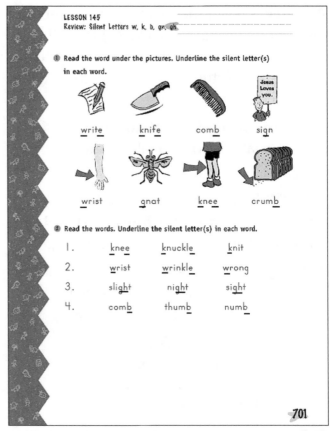

Horizons Kindergarten Phonics

Activity 4. Read the story. Then answer the questions.

1. How old is Wesley? (**five**)
2. What did he have in his knapsack? (**pen**)
3. What person was in his storybook? (**wrestler**)
4. What did Wesley want to learn to do at school? (**read and write**)

Activity 5. Talk to your teacher about what you want most when you are in school. Print a sentence about that on the lines below.

Activity 6. Read one word from each of the rows and have the student put a circle around the correct word in each row.

Words: **written, knife, wrestle
wrap, kitten, knot
thumb, light, sign
knuckle, lamb, wrinkle
gnaw, keep, flight**

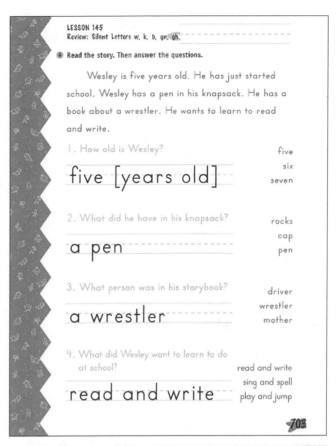

LESSON 145
Review: Silent Letters w, k, b, gn, gh

④ Read the story. Then answer the questions.

Wesley is five years old. He has just started school. Wesley has a pen in his knapsack. He has a book about a wrestler. He wants to learn to read and write.

1. How old is Wesley?

five [years old]

five
six
seven

2. What did he have in his knapsack?

a pen

rocks
cap
pen

3. What person was in his storybook?

a wrestler

driver
wrestler
mother

4. What did Wesley want to learn to do at school?

read and write

read and write
sing and spell
play and jump

703

LESSON 145
Review: Silent Letters w, k, b, gn, gh

⑤ Talk to your teacher about what you want most when you are in school. Print a sentence about that on the lines below.

⑥ Circle the word your teacher reads.

1.	written	knife	wrestle
2.	wrap	kitten	knot
3.	thumb	light	sign
4.	knuckle	lamb	wrinkle
5.	gnaw	keep	flight

704

Lesson 146 - Words Ending in le

Overview

- Introduce words ending in **le**
- Sentence completion
- Story comprehension

Materials and Supplies:

- Teacher's Guide & Student Workbook
- White board
- Reader 4: *The Sunken Bottle*

Teaching Tips:

Use the white board to introduce words ending with **le**. Explain that the **le** makes the sound of **ul** as in **saddle**.

Activity 1&2. Read the words with the teacher. Have the student notice the **le** and the end of each word and the sound it makes. Write the words on the line below each picture.

Pictures: **paddle, candle, bottle
people, kettle, apple
cattle, thimble, pickle
ankle, puddle, jungle
bundle, tumble, bottle**

Activity 3. Read the words together and discuss the meaning of each. Have the student draw a line from the word to the picture it matches. Spell the word below the picture.

Pictures: **jungle, ankle**
candle, bottle
thimble, cattle
people, puddle

Activity 4. Draw a line from the puzzle phrase to the picture.

Pictures: **a saddle on a person**
a rattle on her ankle
a candle on an apple
cattle in a puddle

Activity 5. Read the sentences. Underline the words that end with the letters **le**.

1. My **uncle** asked us a **riddle**.
2. Did you get the new fishing **tackle**?
3. The dogs played in a **puddle** of water.
4. Jack has some **little** kittens that **wiggle** all over.
5. We have a **kettle** on our **table**.
6. Dave's horse has a new **saddle**.

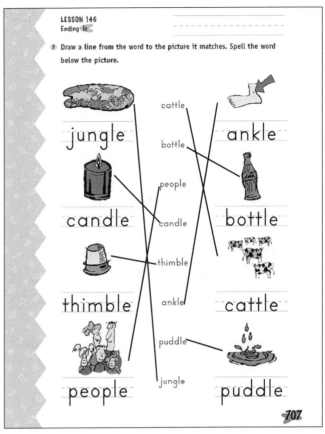

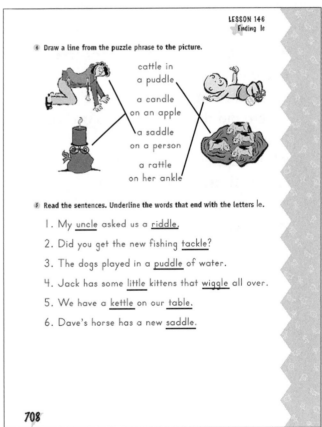

Activity 6. Read the sentences together and discuss the meaning. Have the student choose and print the word from the word bank that goes with the sentence.

Some people can ride horses better if they have a (**saddle**).

A (**kettle**) is used to cook food on the stove or boil water.

You could take a (**tumble**) over a stick and fall down.

If someone fusses about something, we think she will (**grumble**).

The center of something can be the (**middle**).

A (**thimble**) is useful to put on the middle finger when sewing.

Activity 7. Read the story together and discuss its contents. Have the student choose and print the correct answers to the questions.

1. Where did Sam get his horse? (**from his dad**)
2. What did Sam name his horse? (**Shorty**)
3. Where did the horse start to go? (**down the road**)
4. What happened to the horse? (**stumbled**)
5. What happened to Sam? (**fell into a puddle**)

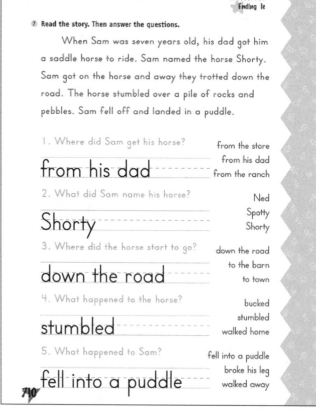

Lesson 147 - Words with all

Overview

- Introduce words with **all**
- Sentence comprehension
- Story comprehension
- Sentence creation

Materials and Supplies:

- Teacher's Guide & Student Workbook
- White board
- Reader 4: *The New Saddle*

Teaching Tip

Use the white board to introduce the ending **all** which makes the sound we hear in the word **ball**.

Activity 1. Read the words together and discuss the meaning. Have the student notice the **all** at the end of each word and the sound it makes. Print the words on the lines below each picture.

   Pictures: **call, fall, hall, tall, wall, small**

Activity 2. Draw a line from the word to the picture it matches. Spell the word under each picture.

   Pictures: **fall, wall, tall, small**

Activity 3. Read the sentences together. Have the student underline the words that have **all** in them.

1. Did Jake catch the **ball** when it came over the house?
2. Jane is as **tall** as her sister.
3. I hope mom will **call** me so I can get to school on time.
4. The little girl can draw on the white **wall**.
5. Bert went to the **mall** to shop.
6. Jim went to first base when he played **baseball**.

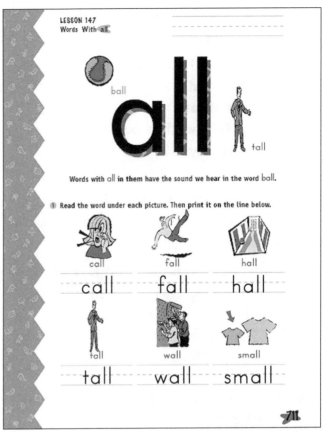

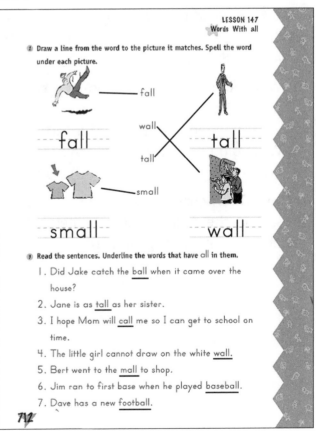

7. Dave has a new **football**.

Horizons Kindergarten Phonics

Activity 4. Draw a line from the puzzle phrase to the picture.

Pictures: **a small elephant with a football**
a tall ant
a fish with a ball
the sky will fall

Activity 5. Read the sentences and words together and discuss the meaning of each. Have the student choose and print the word that completes the sentence.

1. Someone who is not short is (**tall**).
2. We hung a big chart on the (**wall**) of the school.
3. Bob went to first base when he was play-ing (**baseball**).
4. We got wet from the (**rainfall**).
5. Dave got to the goal line when he played (**football**).

Activity 6. Read the story together and dis-cuss the questions. Have the student print the answers on the lines below.

1. Where did Beth and Jane go? (**to the pool**)
2. What happened to Jane? (**she fell**)
3. What did Beth have to do? (**call Dad**)
4. Who came to help? (**her Dad**)

Activity 7. Discuss safety rules of various kinds. Have the student print a sentence that tells about safety and swimming.

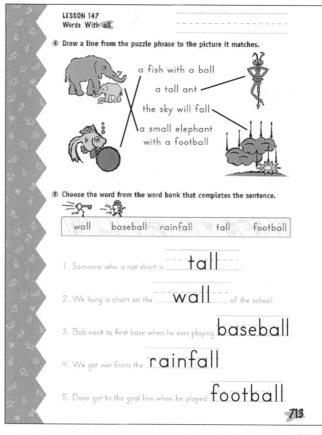

Lesson 148 - Syllables: Double Consonants

Overview

- Introduce syllables
- Division of syllables
- Alphabetical order
- Spelling
- Sentence comprehension
- Story comprehension
- Sentence creation

Materials and Supplies:

- Teacher's Guide & Student Workbook
- White board
- Reader 4: *Mr. Bittle's Helper*

Teaching Tips:

Use the white board to illustrate syllables, showing the division between double consonants as in **kitten**, or between two consonants as in **candy**. Have the student clap the syllables to get the feel of each syllable.

Activity 1. Introduce the Syllable Rule: A syllable is a part of a word spoken as a sound group. A syllable can be divided between double consonants as in kitten, or between two consonants as in candy.

Read the words together and discuss the number of syllables in each. Have the student put a CIRCLE around the words under the pictures that have two syllables with double consonants in the middle.

Pictures: **cattle, button, desk, Daddy, letter, rain, rabbit, dollar**

Activity 2. Read the words together. Have the student put a SQUARE around the words under the pictures that have two syllables divided by two different consonants.

Pictures: **basket, lumber, cow, magnet, lake, dentist, doctor, garden**

Activity 3. Draw a line from the word to the picture it matches.

Pictures: **donkey, valley, bottom, number, window, picnic, cotton, ribbon, candy**

Activity 4. Practice printing words with a double consonant or two different consonants in the middle.

Words: **rabbit, funny, basket, doctor**

Activity 5. Read the sentences together. Have the student underline the words that have a double consonant in the middle.

1. The **rabbit hopped** on the grass.
2. **Daddy** took us to the lake last **summer**.
3. The car drove by the **tunnel** near the main road.
4. The **cattle** were in the barn eating hay.
5. The baby had to have help with the **button** on his coat.

Activity 6. Print the words in alphabetical order.

Words: **apple, button, cotton, tunnel**

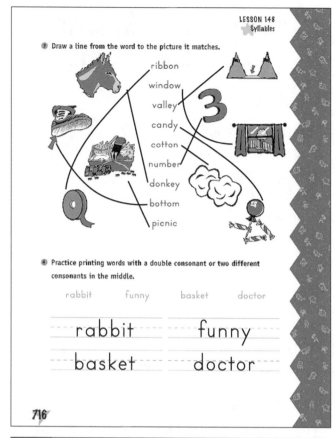

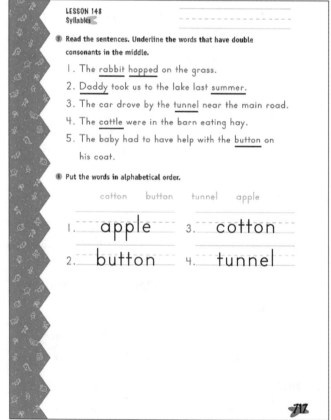

Activity 7. Spell the correct word below each picture. Then print the rest of the words on the lines below.

Pictures: **supper, dollar, letter**

Activity 8. Read the words and sentences together. Have the student choose and print the word to complete the sentence.

1. Some people drink from a (**bottle**), but others want a cup.
2. This (**paddle**) can be used to help row a boat.
3. When he fell in a mud (**puddle**), he got dirty.
4. This red (**apple**) grows on a tree and is good to eat.
5. The girl has a (**ruffle**) on the dress.
6. Ten dimes make one (**dollar**).

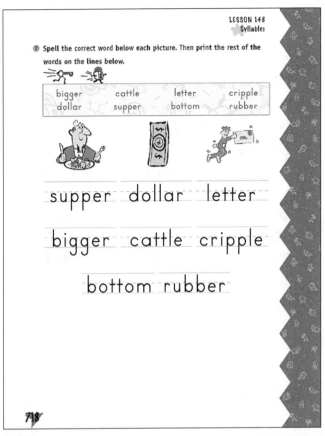

Activity 9. Read the story together. Then have the student answer the questions. Print the answers to the first three questions on the lines below. Talk about the answer to the last question.

1. When did Billy get his bike? **for his birthday**
2. Where did he ride the bike? **around the lake**
3. What happened to the bike? **it was stolen**
4. What should Billy have done? **put his bike away**

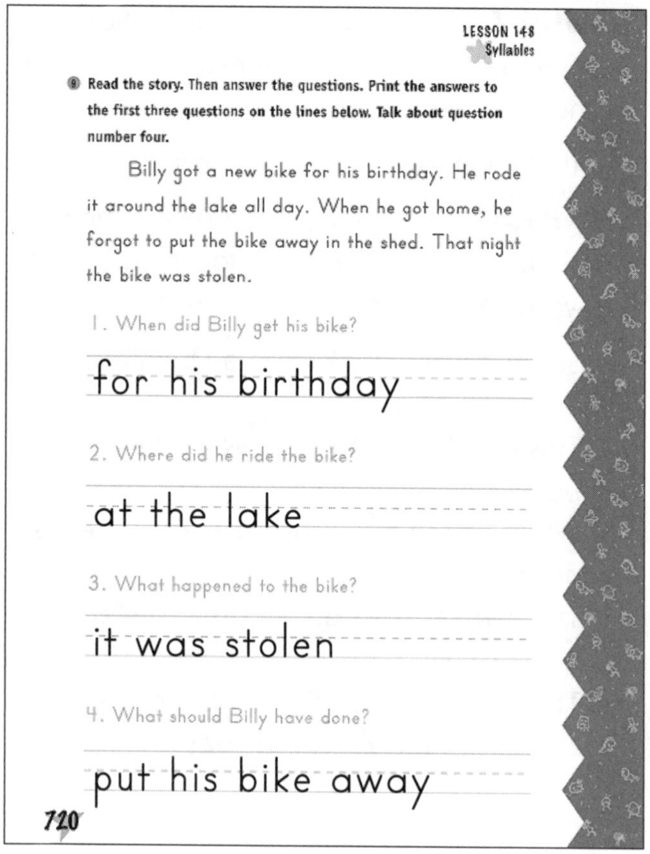

Read the story. Then answer the questions. Print the answers to the first three questions on the lines below. Talk about question number four.

Billy got a new bike for his birthday. He rode it around the lake all day. When he got home, he forgot to put the bike away in the shed. That night the bike was stolen.

1. When did Billy get his bike?

for his birthday

2. Where did he ride the bike?

at the lake

3. What happened to the bike?

it was stolen

4. What should Billy have done?

put his bike away

720

Lesson 149 - Syllables: Compound Words

Overview

- Introduce Compound Words

Materials and Supplies:

- Teacher's Guide & Student Workbook
- White board
- Reader 4: *Skipper's New Name*

Teaching Tips:

Use the white board to illustrate making compound words by combining two words into one. On the board, print two columns of base words and instruct the student to draw lines to show they have merged. Then allow the student to create some make-up compound words by changing the lines.

Activity 1. Introduce the Compound Word Rule: Compound words are made by combining two words into one. Example: **cowboy**. Discuss base words.

Read the words together and discuss the meaning of each. Have the student put a circle around each base word in the compound words below.

Pictures: **mailbox, railroad, snowman, toothbrush, bookcase, ponytail, horseshoe, flagpole**

Activity 2. Read the words together and discuss the meaning as the compound word is made. Have the student draw a line between the two words that make up the compound word in the word bank below.

Words: **lighthouse, herself, upset, downpour, blacksmith without, lifejacket, notebook, eyeball, snowman**

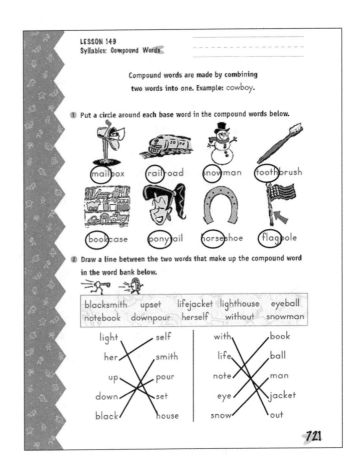

Activity 3. Look at the words under each picture below. Put them together to make a compound word. Print the compound word on the lines below.

Pictures: **football, sunshine**
salesman, airport
grasshopper, upstairs

Activity 4. Look at the words below. CIRCLE all the words that have double consonants in the middle. Put a SQUARE around the compound words.

Double Consonants: **ribbon, kitten, little**
Compound words: **lifejacket, pigtail, northwest, herself, anyone, bookcase, barefoot**

Activity 5. Read the sentences together. Have the student put a circle around the compound word(s) in the sentences.

1. We can go to the lake **anyway**.
2. There was a **downpour** of rain.
3. I do not want to go **without** you.
4. The jet flew into the **airport** at three in the **afternoon**.
5. The **fisherman** got four **catfish** when he was at the lake.
6. We had a fun trip on the **houseboat**.
7. We saw the truck when it had a **blowout** of its tire.
8. Don plays **shortstop** with the **baseball** team.

Activity 6. In your own words tell your teacher what each compound word means.

1. **baseball**
2. **barefoot**
3. **rowboat**
4. **upstairs**
5. **classmate**

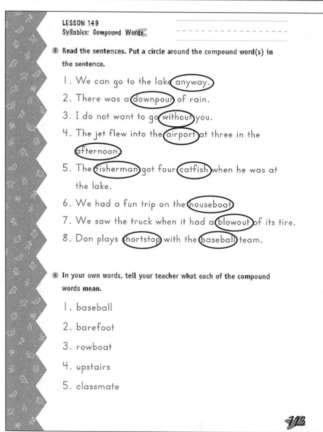

Activity 7. Draw a line from the puzzle phrase to the picture it matches.

Pictures: **a donkey on a runway**
a snowman on a houseboat
a kickstand on a truck
a cat on a flagpole
a catfish with a horseshoe
a football with a hat

Lesson 150 - Syllables: Single Consonant Between Vowels

Overview

- Introduce syllables - single consonant between vowels
- Capitalization and punctuation
- Sequence

Materials and Supplies:

- Teacher's Guide & Student Workbook
- White board
- Reader 4: *Judd's Surprise for Dad*

Teaching Tips:

Use the white board to illustrate the division of syllables with a single consonant between vowels. Review capitalization and punctuation.

Activity 1. Introduce the rule: A single consonant between vowels usually goes with the second vowel. Example: **ti–ger, wa–ter**. Read the words together and discuss the meaning of each. Have the student notice where the single consonant rule applies.

Pictures: **spider, girl, police, hotel, parade, radar, farm, baby, vacant, alone, tame, pirate**

Activity 2. Read the words in the word bank together. Have the student choose and print the words below the picture. Underline the one consonant between the vowels and show that it goes with the second syllable.

Pictures: pa**r**ade, pi**l**ot, ce**m**ent
ti**g**er, spi**d**er, ba**b**y

Activity 3. Read one word from each of the rows and have the student put a circle around the correct word in each row.

Words: **tiger, trees, trade**

spider, safe, sift
pirate, pain, pick
radar, roof, rain

Activity 4. Draw a line from the puzzle phrase to the picture.

Phrases: **a pig with a basket**
a spider in a pocket
a pirate in pain
a tiger with a dentist

Activity 5. Read the sentences together. Have the student underline the words that have two syllables.

1. The **pilot** met us at the **airport**.
2. How **many** teeth does a **tiger** have?
3. How **many** legs does a **spider** have?
4. Ron put the eggs in a **basket**.
5. The **water** is **frozen** in the pond.
6. Dad used **lumber** to make a shed.

Activity 6. Look at the pictures and discuss sequencing. Have the student print (1) under the one that happens first, (2) under the next one, and (3) under the one that would happen last.

Pictures: **Girl puts on her coat.**
Girl and dad walk to the car.
Girl and dad drive to zoo.

Activity 7. Review capitalization and punctuation. Read the sentences together and have the student print the sentences below.

Janet will go to the dentist**.**
Will you see a tiger at the zoo**?**

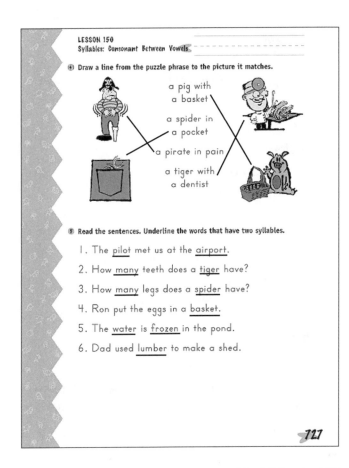

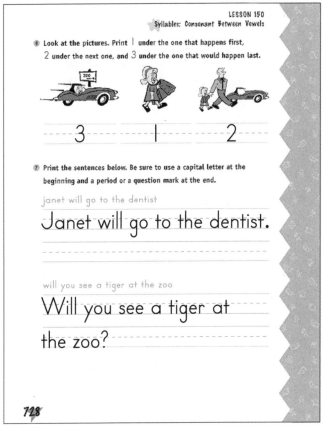

Lesson 151 - Review Syllables

Overview

- Review syllables
- Sentence completion
- Creative writing

Materials and Supplies:

- Teacher's Guide & Student Workbook
- White board
- Reader 4: *Silly Farmer Tallman*

Teaching Tips:

Review the lesson covering the pictures, words, and sentences together. Allow the student to work as independently as possible. Make note if there is an area that may need reinforcement.

Activity 1. Put a CIRCLE around the compound words under the pictures:

Pictures: **basketball, candy, aircraft, pocket, ponytail, mailbox, basket, baseball**

Activity 2. Put a SQUARE around the two-syllable words that are NOT compound words.

Pictures: **airport, window, valley, grasshopper, bottom, sunshine, picnic, lumber**

Activity 3. Underline the two-syllable words that have a single consonant between the vowels.

Pictures: **tiger, summer, hotel, rattle, pocket, water, bubble, spider**

Activity 4. Draw a line from the word to the picture it matches.

Pictures: **football, beehive, rattle, rowboat, birthday, baseball**

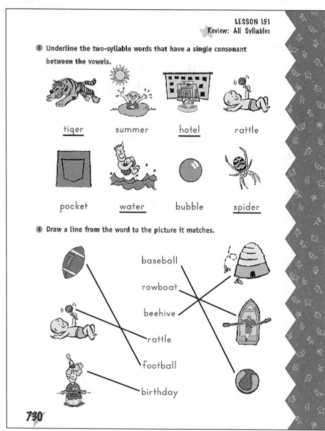

Activity 5. Choose and print the correct word on the lines in each sentence.

1. The (**cattle**) are in the barnyard.
2. Janet put the eggs in a (**basket**) on the table.
3. Jack put a (**bridle**) on the horse so he could lead it.
4. The monkey lived in a (**jungle**).
5. The little rocks looked like (**pebbles**).

Activity 6. Think of some compound words you know. Talk to your teacher and print a sentence of your own using a compound word.

Activity 7. Think of some words that have a double consonant in the middle. Talk to your teacher and print your own sentence on a sheet of paper.

Activity 8. Look at the words in the word bank. Choose and print a word on the line that would make the sentence correct.

1. The money that is the same as ten dimes is a (**dollar**).
2. Houses are often made of (**lumber**).
3. When you are sick, you see a (**doctor**).
4. Baby Jane drinks her milk from a (**bottle**).
5. Most people like to watch a good (**football**) game.
6. When we go to the zoo, we like to see the (**tigers**).
7. A shirt often has six (**buttons**).

Lesson 152 - Suffix: -ing Endings

Overview

- Introduce Suffix - **ing** ending
- Introduce prepositions
- Sentence completion

Materials and Supplies:

- Teacher's Guide & Student Workbook
- White board
- Reader 4: *The Wrestlers*

Teaching Tips:

Use the white board to illustrate adding the suffix -**ing** to a base word.

Activity 1. Explain that suffixes are word segments at the end of a word. A suffix can change or add meaning to the base word. Example: **boss – bossing; sell – selling**

Read the words together and have the student print each word on the lines below.

Pictures: **fixing, buzzing, bucking, yelling, camping, kissing**

Activity 2. Read the words together and discuss the meaning of each. Have the student draw a line from the word to the picture it matches. Spell the word below the picture.

Pictures: **bunking, asking docking, dumping fishing, bending dusting, mixing**

Activity 3. Read the sentences together adding **ing**. Have the student fill in the blank spaces in each base word with **ing**. Reread the sentence and underline the base word.

1. My dad is **fix**ing the roof on the house.
2. Jan is **look**ing at the money in her bank.
3. The gang is **yell**ing at the football game.
4. We will go **fish**ing at the lake.
5. The lady is **sell**ing rings at the store.
6. All the kids are **duck**ing under the bar.
7. Two cars were **bump**ing into each other.
8. The man with the cane was **limp**ing.
9. We set up the tent when we went **camp**ing.

Activity 4. Introduce the Preposition Rule: A preposition is a word that connects parts of the sentence such as **in** the house, **by** the stove, and **from** the girl. Study the pictures and sentences together. Have the student draw a line to the prepositional phrase that tells about the picture.

1. The fish were (**in the fishbowl**.)
2. Three books were (**on the shelf**.)
3. Sam sat (**on the swing**.)
4. Mom fixed dinner (**at six o'clock**.)

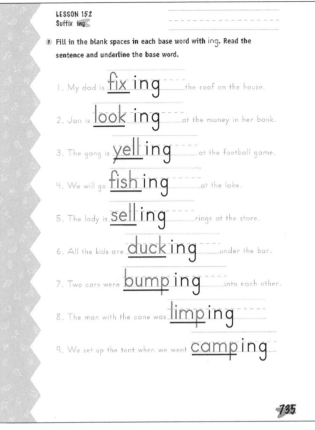

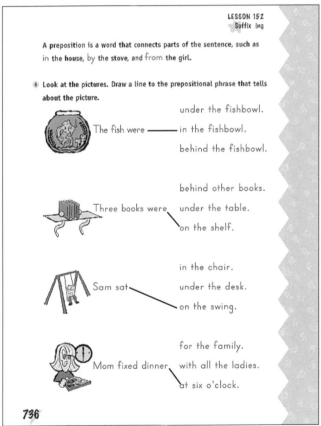

Activity 5 & 6. Study the pictures and read the sentences together. Have the student underline the preposition that connects the sentence.

The boy sits **on** a chair.
My dog puts his bone **in** the dirt.
Jan has her feet **under** the table.
Did you look for your toy **behind** the couch?

The bird's nest is **inside** the birdhouse.
The cats tail is curved **around** his neck.
Mom will fix dinner **for** six people.
We put the cups **above** the middle shelf.

5 Look at the pictures below. Underline the preposition that connects the sentence.

The boy sits on a chair.

My dog puts his bone in the dirt

Jan has her feet under the table

Did you look for your toy behind the couch?

737

6 Look at the pictures below. Underline the preposition that connects the sentence.

The bird's nest is inside the birdhouse.

The cat's tail is curved around his neck.

Mom will fix dinner for six people.

We put the mugs above the middle shelf.

738

Lesson 153 - Soft c

Overview

- Introduce Soft **c**
- Sentence completion
- Review nouns

Materials and Supplies:

- Teacher's Guide & Student Workbook
- White board
- Reader 4: *The Dancing Elephants*

Teaching Tips:

Introduce the Soft **c** Rule: When **c** is followed by **e, i, or y,** the **c** is called soft and makes the sound of **ssss**. Example: **city, cent, cycle, face.**

Activity 1. Use the white board to introduce words with soft **c**. Have the student note the vowel following the **c**. Read the words together under each picture and discuss the meaning. Print the word on the line below.

Pictures: **ace, ice, center, pencil, fence, city**

Activity 2. Read the words together and discuss the meaning of each. Have the student draw a line from the word to the picture it matches. Spell the words below each picture.

Pictures: **slice, pounce ocelot, fence prince, celery**

Activity 3. Review nouns that are persons, places, or things. Instruct the student to print two nouns for each. Answers will vary.

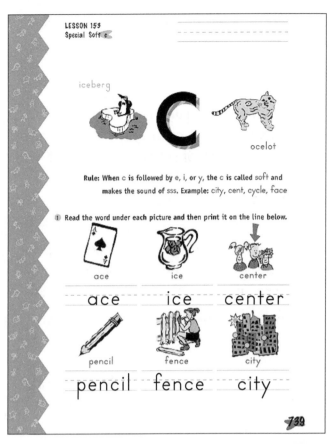

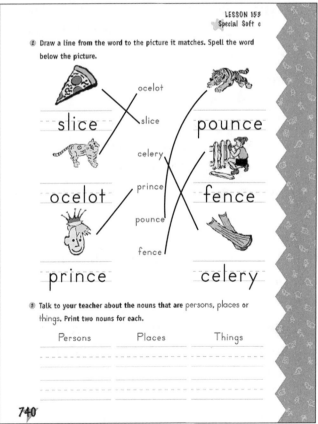

Activity 4. Read the sentences below. Have the student underline the word(s) in each sentence that has the soft **c** sound.

1. Fran drove to the **city** in her new car.
2. We will have a **race** to the **fence**.
3. Did you draw a **circle** on your paper?
4. I have an **ace** of spades in my hand.
5. Mom fixed **rice** for dinner.
6. The road was **icy** from the frost.

Activity 5. Read the sentences and words together. Have the student choose and print one of the words in the word bank to complete the sentence.

1. An airplane takes up a lot of (**space**).
2. The (**price**) of the car was too much to pay.
3. There were three baby (**mice**) in a cage.
4. The music was so good I wanted to (**dance**).

Activity 6. Read the words together. Have the student choose six of the words below to learn to spell. Print them on the lines below.

Words: **race, grace, face
place, lace, nice
spicy, fancy, fence
cedar, celery, circus
city, twice, dance**

Activity 7. Review Rule: A noun is the name of a person, place, or thing. Read the sentences together. Have the student underline the nouns in each sentence. Count the number of nouns and write it in the space at the end of the sentence.

1. **Bob** took his **horses** to the **barn**. (3)
2. **Beth** went to **town** to see a **show**. (3)
3. The **fish** were swimming in the **pond**. (2)
4. **Bill** wants to go **home**. (2)
5. **Dad** cooked **dinner**. (2)

Horizons Kindergarten Phonics

Lesson 154 - Soft g

Overview

- Introduce Soft **g**
- Alphabetical order
- Sentence comprehension
- Sequence

Materials and Supplies:

- Teacher's Guide & Student Workbook
- White board
- Reader 4: *The Giant*

Teaching Tips:

Use the white board to illustrate the Soft **g** Rule: When **g** is followed by **e, i, or y**, the **g**, is called soft **g** and makes the sound of **j** as in **cage** or **giant**.

Activity 1. Introduce the Soft **g** Rule. Study the words and pictures together and discuss the meaning of each. Have the student take note of the placement of the vowel in connection with the **g** in each word. Print the words on the lines below the pictures.

Pictures: **gem, dodge, large giant, judge, range**

Activity 2. Read the words and study the pictures together. Have the student draw a line from the word to the picture it matches. Finish spelling the word below the picture by filling in the **dge**.

Pictures: ba**dge**, ju**dge**, smu**dge**, fu**dge** he**dge**, bri**dge**, ri**dge**, do**dge**

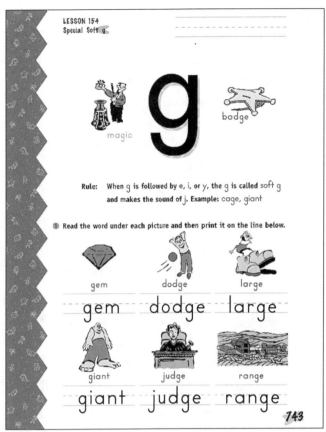

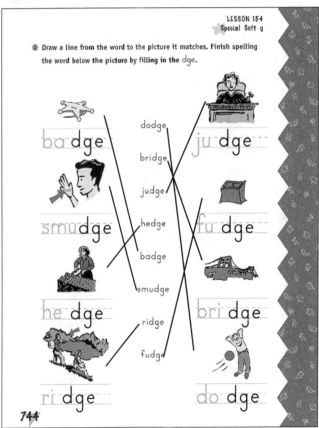

Activity 3. Read the words and study the pictures together. Have the student notice the placement of the **g** and the vowel following to complete the spelling of each of the words. Draw a line from the word to the picture it matches. Finish spelling the word below the picture by filling in the **g** in the middle of the word.

Pictures: **gadget, Ginger, magic, fidget**

Activity 4. Put the words in alphabetical order.

Words: **basket, comb, giraffe, land**

Activity 5. Read the words together and discuss the sound of **g** in each word. Have the student print the words in the columns below. Explain that occasionally there are exceptions to the rule, as in the word **gift**.

soft **g** as in **cage**: **hinge, badge, giraffe**

hard **g** as in **gate**: **gift, goat, bum**

Activity 6. Read the sentences together. Have the student underline the word(s) in each sentence that has the soft **g** sound.

1. Will **Ginger manage** when her mom is not at home?
2. We put the car on a **huge barge**.
3. The farmer had cattle on the **range**.
4. The school went to zoo to see the **giraffe**.
5. **Gene** was on the **stage** at school.

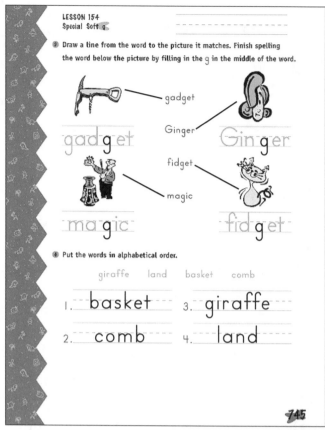

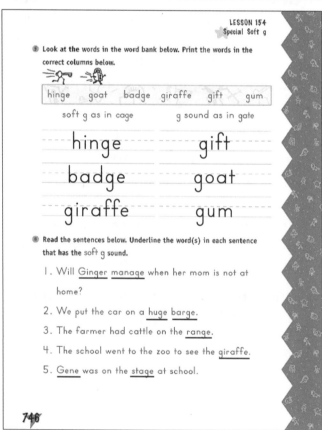

Lesson 155 – Review: Suffix -ing; Soft c and g

Overview

- Review Suffix **-ing**
- Review Soft **c**
- Review Soft **g**
- Creative writing

Materials and Supplies:

- Teacher's Guide & Student Workbook
- White board
- Reader 4: *A Hospital for Vance*

Teaching Tips:

As in all review lessons, read the words and study the pictures together. Have the student work as independently as possible. Make note of any areas in which reinforcement is needed.

Activity 1. Read the base words in the word bank. Print the words below by adding **-ing** to them. Underline the base word.

Words: **camp**ing, **fix**ing, **add**ing, **cast**ing
bending, **sell**ing, **box**ing, **catch**ing

Activity 2. From the words in the word bank, choose and print the word to make the sentence correct.

1. The baby was (**spilling**) his milk all over his crib.
2. We can hear the (**blasting**) of the bomb.
3. Meg keeps (**brushing**) her hair so it stays nice.
4. Mom was (**chilling**) the pudding so it would stay cool.
5. The truck will be (**dumping**) trash all day.
6. Is Janet (**filling**) the glass too full of milk?

Activity 3. Soft **c** review. Sometimes **c** sounds like **s**. Circle the correct word in each box that names the picture.

Pictures: **celery, circle, city, cent**

Activity 4. From the words in the word bank, choose and print the word to make the sentence correct.

1. Five (**cents**) is the same as a nickel.
2. I like to eat (**celery**) with my dinner.
3. The (**circus**) animals were eating their food.
4. I hope we do not have to move to a big (**city**).
5. Marge had a nice dress for the (**dance**).

Activity 5. Review Soft **g**. Sometimes **g** sounds like **j**. Circle the correct word in each box that names the picture.

Pictures: **giraffe, badge, giant, gem**

Activity 6. From the words in the word bank, choose and print the word to make the sentence correct.

1. This man is so big, he looks like a (**giant**).
2. This man is so little, he looks like a (**midget**).
3. They loaded the boats on the (**barge**).
4. Gene drove the car over the (**bridge**).
5. The man on stage did some (**magic**) tricks.

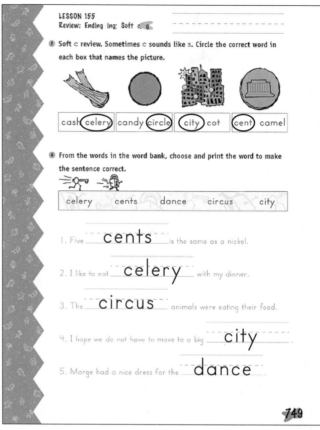

Activity 7. Read all three sentences in the mini story. Put a 1 on the line under the sentence that should come first in the story. Put a **2** under the sentence that comes next, and **3** under the sentence that would be last in the story.

1. **Bill was getting ready for the race.**
2. **Bill ran fast and won the race.**
3. **The judge gave Bill a badge for winning.**

Activity 8. Study the pictures and discuss sequencing. Have the student put 1 under the one that happens first, 2 under the next one, and 3 under the one that would happen last.

1. **Dad went to the store in his car.**
2. **Dad bought a gem for Mom.**
3. **Dad gave the gem to Mom.**

Activity 9. Read the phrases together. Discuss the words for vocabulary development. Draw a line from the puzzle phrase to the picture.

Phrases: **a badge on a giraffe**
a gerbil with a goose
a giant in a rage
a gypsy in a cage

Activity 10. Look at the table with food on it. Talk to your teacher about the foods you like to eat. Print a sentence about what kinds of food keep you healthy.

Lesson 156 - Non-Phonetic: ph, alk

Overview

- Introduce Non-phonetic **ph**, **alk**
- Sentence comprehension
- Introduce contractions

Materials and Supplies:

- Teacher's Guide & Student Workbook
- White board
- Reader 4: *Elephants*

Teaching Tips:

When introducing the non-phonetic words, use the white board to illustrate. In words with **ph**, have the student cross out the **ph** and superimpose the letter **f** so they become aware of the change in sounds. Have the student notice that the **ph** may come at the beginning, middle, or end of a word.

Activity 1. Introduce the Rule: The letter combination of **ph** has the sound of **f**. Example: **photo** sounds like **foto**.

Read the words and study the pictures together. Discuss the meaning of the words. Have the student read the words again under each picture and then print it on the line.

Pictures: **phone, photo, gopher, elephant, trophy, earphone**

Activity 2. Read the words and study the pictures together. Discuss the meaning of each word for vocabulary development. Have the student draw a line from the word to the picture it matches. Spell the word under each picture.

Pictures: **elephant, Philip, gopher, earphone, typhoon, trophy**

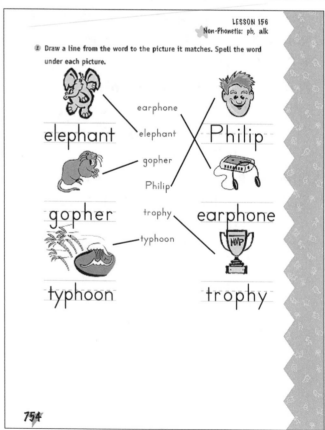

120

Activity 3. Introduce the rule: Contractions are single words made by putting two words together, but taking out a letter or letters. An apostrophe (') is always used where the letter or letters have been left out.

Read the words together and discuss the formation of the contraction. Have the student underline the letter that has to be left out to make the contraction.

Words:
do n**o**t	don't
have n**o**t	haven't
is n**o**t	isn't
does n**o**t	doesn't
was n**o**t	wasn't
were n**o**t	weren't

Activity 4. Crisscross the words to match the contraction.

Words:
do not	**don't**
is not	**isn't**
can not	**can't**
have not	**haven't**
does not	**doesn't**
were not	**weren't**

Activity 5. Read the two words that make the contraction. Read the contraction. Underline the letters that have to be left out to make the contraction.

Words:
I **ha**ve	I've
we **ha**ve	we've
she **wi**ll	she'll
he **wi**ll	he'll
they **wi**ll	they'll
it **is**	it's

Activity 6. Talk to your teacher about using a contraction. Think of a sentence about something you can do. Then change it to a sentence about something you can't do. Print it on a piece of paper.

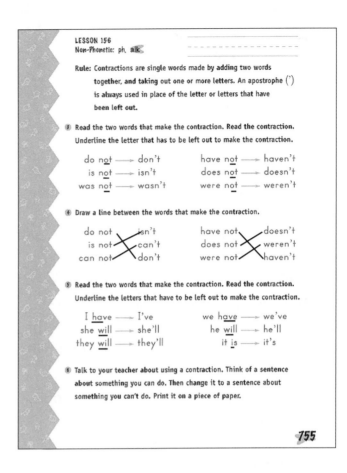

Activity 7. Read the sentences. Print a contraction on the blank in place of the two other words.

1. I have not seen the moon tonight. (**haven't**)
2. John does not like to play football. (**doesn't**)
3. Dad is not going to jaywalk on the street. (**isn't**)
4. The baby can not talk yet. (**can't**)
5. I do not have any chalk in my box. (**don't**)

Activity 8. Read the sentences and words together and discuss the meanings. Have the student choose the word from the word bank that describes the sentence.

1. This is a narrow board on which people walk. (**catwalk**)
2. It is illegal to walk across the street this way. (**jaywalk**)
3. This is the right place to walk when you are in town. (**sidewalk**)

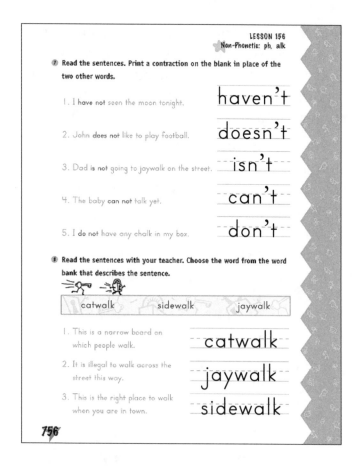

Activity 9. Read the sentences and words together. Discuss the meaning of each. Have the student choose the sentence that describes the word from the word bank. Print the word on the line.

1. We saw pictures of the bad storm. (**typhoon**)
2. This huge animal lives in the zoo. (**elephant**)
3. I am glad we have one so I can talk to my friends. (**phone**)
4. The boys looked like twins in the picture. (**photo**)
5. A part of the family can be this relative. (**nephew**)
6. This person doesn't have a family. (**orphan**)
7. This large animal swims in the sea. (**dolphin**)

Horizons Kindergarten Phonics

Activity 10. Introduce the non-phonetic rule: Parts of some words do not follow the phonetic rules, but they do have their own sound. Example: Words with **alk** in them have the sound we hear in the word **walk**.

Read the words and study the pictures together. Discuss the meaning of each word. Have the student print the word under each picture.

Pictures: **talk, walk, chalk**

Activity 11. Read the words and study the pictures. Have the student draw a line from the picture to the word it matches.

Pictures: **catwalk, sidewalk, jaywalk, stalk**

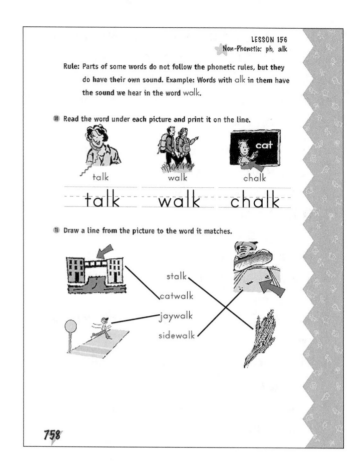

Lesson 157 - Non-Phonetic: old, olst, olt

Overview

- Introduce Non Phonetic **old, ost, olt**
- Sentence comprehension
- Introduce action verbs
- Creative writing

Materials and Supplies:

- Teacher's Guide & Student Workbook
- White board
- Reader 4: *The Monarch Butterfly*

Teaching Tips:

Use the white board to illustrate the non-phonetic words with **old, ost, olt**. Have the student note that even though there is only one vowel in the word, it makes the long vowel sound.

In introducing action verbs, have the student read the words and then act them out in demonstration.

Activity 1. Introduce the non-phonetic words with **old, olt, ost**. Rule: Parts of some words do not follow the phonetic rules. They have their own sound. Even though there is only one vowel in the word, it makes the long vowel sound.

Read the words and study the pictures together. Discuss the meaning of each word. Have the student read the word again under each picture and then print it on the line.

Pictures: **colt, bolt, post,**
       fold, sold, hostess

Activity 2. Read the words and study the pictures together. Have the student draw a line from the word to the picture it matches. Spell the word under the picture.

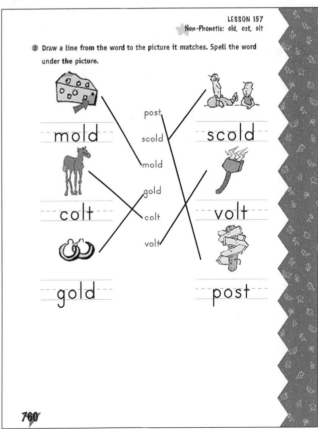

Pictures: **mold, scold**
      colt, volt
      gold, post

Activity 3. Read the sentences and words together. Discuss the various meanings. Have the student choose the sentence that describes the word from the word bank. Print the word on the line.

1. The food was left because the man didn't sell it. (**unsold**)
2. The story is about something that isn't real. (**ghost**)
3. Men got rich when they dug in the ground for it. (**gold**)
4. Its fun to have a baby horse on the farm. (**colt**)
5. They needed a high one to hang the telephone wires. (**post**)
6. Chickens lose their feathers each year. (**molt**)

Activity 4. Introduce the rule: A verb is a word that shows action or state of being.

Read the words and study the pictures. Have the student demonstrate the action with each action verb. Read the words again and print them on the lines below the picture.

Pictures: **run, jump, push
ride, play, lost
sleep, stop, throw**

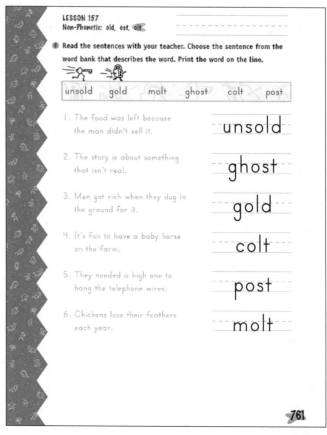

Activity 5. Read the sentences and words together. Discuss the meaning. Have the student choose an action verb from the word bank to complete each sentence. Print the word on the blank in the sentence.

1. Bill will (**fight**) in the boxing ring.
2. Both of the boys will (**play**) ball on the team.
3. I can (**run**) the foot race and win.
4. The baby (**lost**) his shoe.
5. The pony let us (**ride**) horseback every day.
6. At night we all go to (**sleep**) in our own beds.

Activity 6. Talk to your teacher about action verbs. Demonstrate how a person can run, jump, trot, sleep, stop. Print a sentence using one of the action verbs.

Activity 7. Read the sentences and study the pictures together. Discuss the verbs. Have the student underline the action verb in each sentence.

1. The school kids **flew** their kites at noon.
2. The baby sleeps in her crib.
3. Hank **struck** the wall with his car.
4. The vase **broke** into five parts.
5. Jack **ate** all the apple pie.
6. We **march** in most parades.

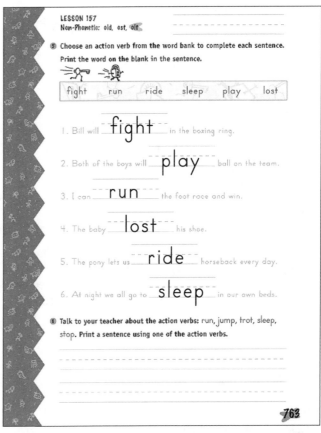

Lesson 158 - Non-Phonetic: ild, ind

Overview:

- Introduce Non Phonetic **ild, ind**
- Sentence completion
- Review Nouns
- Introduce Pronouns
- Verbs
- Creative Writing

Materials and Supplies:

- Teacher's Guide & Student Workbook
- White board
- Reader 4: *Jake's Paper Route*

Teaching Tips:

Use the white board to illustrate the non-phonetic words with **ind**, and **ild**. Have the student note that even though there is only one vowel in the word, it makes the long vowel sound. Review nouns and introduce pronouns as taking the place of a noun. On the white board list pronouns: **he**, **she**, **they**, **we**, **us**, **him**, **her**, and discuss the relationship to the nouns.

Activity 1. Introduce the non-phonetic words with **ild** and **ind**. Rule: Parts of some words do not follow the phonetic rules. They have their own sound. Even though there is only one vowel in the word, it makes the long vowel sound.

Read the words and study the pictures together. Discuss the meaning of each word. Have the student read the word again under each picture and then print it on the line.

Pictures: **wild, mild, wind, child, kind, mind, blind, grind**

Activity 2. Read the words and study the pictures together. Have the student draw a line from the word to the picture it matches. Spell the word under the picture.

128

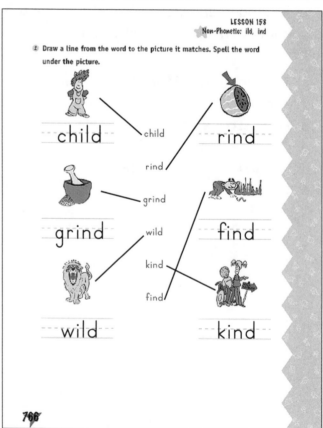

Pictures: **child, rind, grind, find, wild, kind**

Activity 3. Read the sentences and words together. Have the student choose and print the correct word to complete the sentence.

1. The animals in the zoo are (**wild**).
2. Today when the sun was shining, it felt so (**mild**) and nice.
3. We knew the lady was (**blind**) when we saw her white cane.
4. The dentist had to (**grind**) this tooth first.
5. The (**child**) played on the swings in the park.

Activity 4. Introduce pronouns as taking the place of a noun. Read the sentences together and substitute the name of a person(s) that would be appropriate for the sentence. Have the student underline the pronouns in each sentence.

1. **She** will go to school with **her** brother.
2. **He** can play in the yard with the dog.
3. **They** want to go to a show.
4. **We** will take the bus to town.

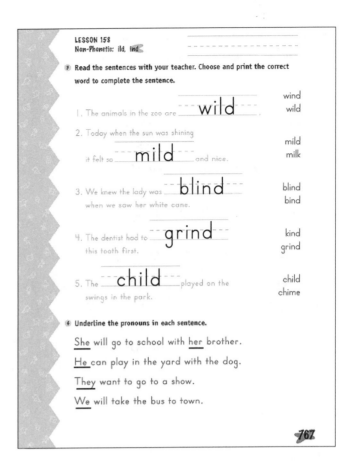

Activity 5. Review nouns again. Read the sentences together. Have the student put a circle around the nouns in the sentences. On the line at the end of the sentence print if the noun is (1) name of a person, (2) name of a thing, or (3) name of a place.

1. The **dog** sleeps all day. (**2**)
2. **Jack** likes to read. (**1**)
3. **Park Street** has been snowy this winter. (**3**)
4. **Fran** and **Phil** are nice. (**1**)

Activity 6. Review action verbs. Read the sentences together and allow the student to act out some of the verbs in the sentences. Put a square around the action verbs in the sentences.

Joe **caught** the baseball.
Jan and Fred **walked** to school.
The dog **jumps** high to get the ball.
How many fish **swim** in your tank?
We always **stop** at a stop sign.

Activity 7. Have the student discuss his own sentence. Think of a noun and what is happening. Think: who (noun or pronoun) did what (action verb). Be sure to put a capital letter for the beginning word and finish it with the correct punctuation mark. Instruct the student to use a separate sheet of paper for this exercise.

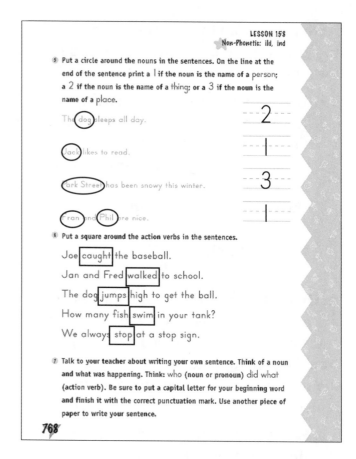

Lesson 159 - Review: Non-Phonetic Words

Overview

- Review Non-Phonetic words
- Spelling
- Sentence completion
- Word search
- Puzzle

Materials and Supplies:

- Teacher's Guide & Student Workbook
- White board
- Reader 4: *Rodney's Jobs*

Teaching Tips:

As in all review lessons, read the words and study the pictures together. Have the student work as independently as possible. Make note of any areas in which reinforcement is needed.

Activity 1. Look at the pictures. Choose a word from the word bank and print it under the picture it matches.

    Pictures: **gopher, colt, blind**
                 gold, child, phone
                 hostess, elephant

Activity 2. Draw a line from the word to the picture it matches. Then spell the word below each picture.

    Pictures: **earphones, orphan**
                 elephant, trophy
                 grind, Philip
                 photo, mind

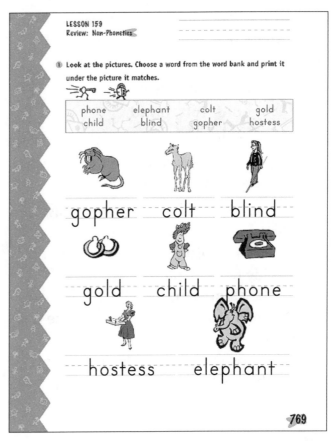

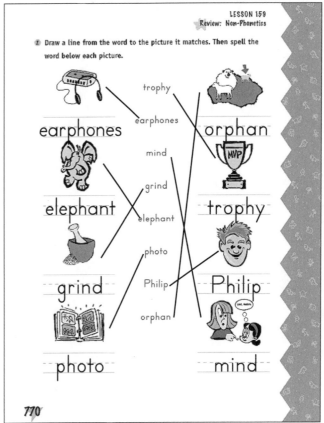

Activity 3. Circle the missing letters in each word. Write the missing letters on the lines below the picture.

Pictures: w**ild**, s**old**, f**ind**,
g**old**, c**olt**, gr**ind**,
f**old**, bl**ind**

Activity 4. Use the words in the word bank to complete each sentence.

1. Jan was (**kind**) to the lady who was blind.
2. The little (**child**) was asleep in her crib.
3. A baby horse is a (**colt**).
4. I hope I (**find**) my lost shoe.
5. Dad had to (**grind**) the feed for the cattle.
6. Mom will (**hold**) the baby in her arms for the photo.

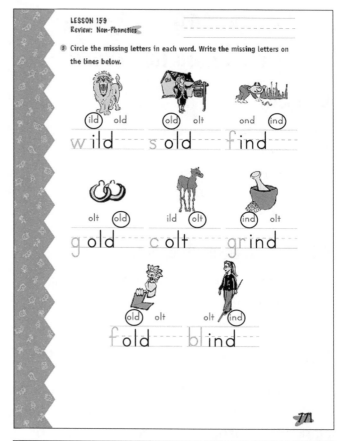

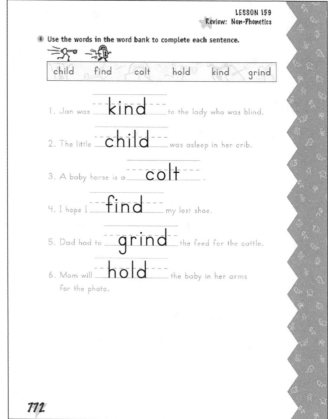

Activity 5. Circle the words in the puzzle that are in the word bank.

Words across: **child, find, hold,**
Words down: **colt, kind, grind**

Activity 6. Read the review words for your teacher.

1. **football, dollar, kitten**
2. **spider, basket, fixing**
3. **slice, race, giant**
4. **elephant, child, blind**
5. **mailbox, upstairs, catfish**
6. **banking, nice, pencil**
7. **large, tiger, phone**
8. **mind, colt, cold**
9. **most, told, wild**

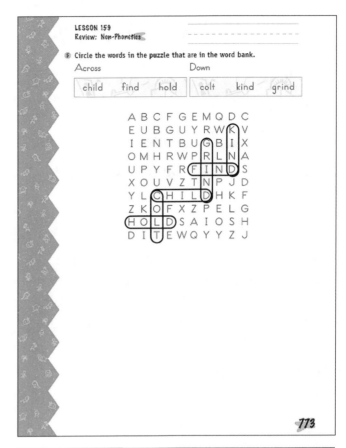

⑤ Circle the words in the puzzle that are in the word bank.

Across | Down

| child | find | hold | colt | kind | grind |

```
A B C F G E M Q D C
E U B G U Y R W K V
I E N T B U G B I X
O M H R W P R L N A
U P Y F R F I N D S
X O U V Z T N P J D
Y L C H I L D H K F
Z K O F X Z P E L G
H O L D S A I O S H
D I T E W Q Y Y Z J
```

113

⑥ Read the review words for your teacher.

1.	football	dollar	kitten
2.	spider	basket	fixing
3.	slice	race	giant
4.	elephant	child	blind
5.	mailbox	upstairs	catfish
6.	banking	nice	pencil
7.	large	tiger	phone
8.	mind	colt	cold
9.	most	told	wild

114

Lesson 160 - Review

Overview

- Review - All

Materials and Supplies:

- Teacher's Guide & Student Workbook
- White board

Teaching Tips:

As in all review lessons, read the words together and study the pictures. Have the student word as independently as possible. Make note of any areas in which reinforcement is needed.

Activity 1. Choose the correct letters and spell the words under the pictures.

> Pictures: c**or**n, d**ar**k, sk**ir**t
>
> sp**ar**k, sh**ir**t, f**or**k

Activity 2. Put a CIRCLE around the words that have the sound of long **a**. Put a SQUARE around the words that have the sound of long **e**.

> long **a**: **hay, day, x-ray, play, stay, tray, pray**
>
> long **e**: **monkey, key, donkey**

Activity 3. Choose the correct letters and spell the words under the pictures. Explain to the students that some of the words are **not** plural words and do not require an **s** or an **es** at the end.

> Pictures: cat**s**, church**es**, ship**s**, ship, house, peach**es**, sled**s**, box**es**, watch**es**, brush**es**, toy, dog**s**

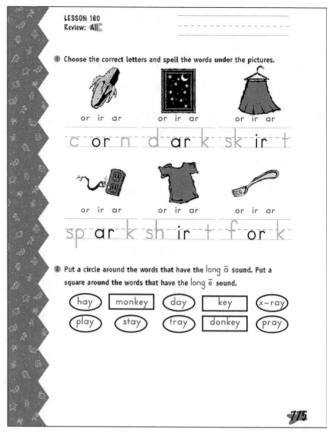

Activity 4. Choose the correct letters and spell the words under the picture. Use **y** or change the **y** to **i** and add **es**. Some words are **not** plural and do not require an **i** or an **ies**.

Pictures: bab**ies**, lad**ies**, kitty,
puppy, cherr**ies**, dais**ies**

Activity 5. Read the words. Put a line between the double consonants in the middle.

Words: **but/ton, fun/ny, rab/bit, let/ter, rub/ber**

Activity 6. Read the words. Put a line between the two syllables divided by two different consonants.

Words: **bas/ket, har/bor, num/ber, six/teen, win/dow**

Activity 7. Choose the correct letters and spell the words under the pictures.

Pictures: qu**ee**n, c**oa**t, g**oa**t
ch**ai**n, r**ai**n, tr**ee**

Activity 8. Put a circle around the pictures that have the letter **y** that makes the sound of long **i**.

Pictures: **cry, fly, train, dry**

Activity 9. Put a SQUARE around the pictures that have the letter **y** that makes the sound of long **e**.

Pictures: **gray, candy, skinny, puppy**

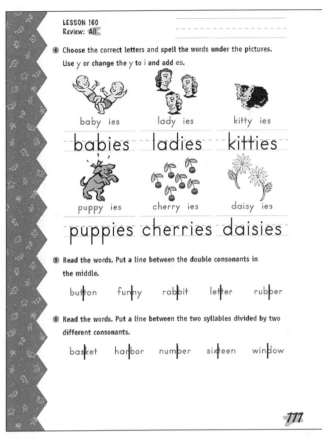

Activity 10. Draw a line from the picture to the word it matches.

  Pictures: **clown, mouth, stool, town, crow**

Activity 11. Draw a line from the picture to the word it matches.

  Pictures: **cloud, elbow, brook, tooth, brown**

Activity 12. Draw a line from the picture to the word it matches.

  Pictures: **Paul, claw, prawn, vault, shawl, auto**

Activity 13. Draw a line from the picture to the word it matches.

  Pictures: **cowboy, flew, joint, coin, threw, toy**

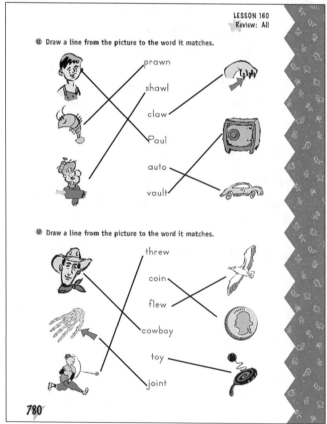

Horizons Kindergarten Phonics

Activity 14. Read the words. Cross out the silent letters in each word. Draw a line to the picture it matches.

Pictures: **knife, comb, knee, wrist, write**

Activity 15. Read the words. Cross out the silent letters in each word. Draw a line to the picture it matches.

Pictures: **night, crumb, right, sign, gnat**

Activity 16. Crisscross the words to make compound words. Print the words on the lines below.

Words: **mailbox, bookcase, horseshoe flagpole, toothbrush, sunshine**

Activity 17. Put a circle around the words that have the sound of soft **c** or **g**.

Words: **cent, crate, price, prince, flat goat, celery, range, giant, badge**

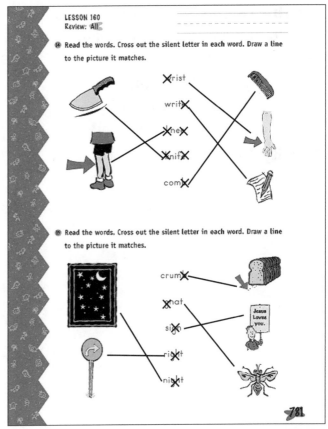

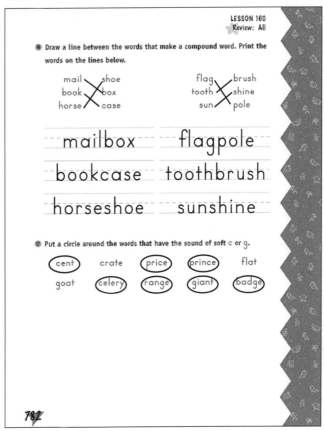

Activity 18. Look at the pictures. Choose a word from the word bank and print it under the picture it matches.

Pictures: **sold, photo, blind**
child, trophy, tight
phone, jaywalk, colt

Activity 19. Draw a picture of yourself.